WHERE'S THE SHORTAGE?

A NONTECHNICAL GUIDE TO PETROLEUM ECONOMICS

BY BOB TIPPEE

WHERE'S THE SHORTAGE?

A NONTECHNICAL GUIDE TO PETROLEUM ECONOMICS

PennWell Books

PennWell Publishing Company
Tulsa, Oklahoma

Library of Congress Cataloging-in-Publication Data

Tippee, Bob.
    Where's the shortage?: a nontechnical guide to
petroleum economics / by Bob Tippee.
        p.   cm.
    Includes bibliographical references.
    ISBN 0-87814-403-X
1. Petroleum industry and trade. 2. Petroleum
products — Prices.
3. Organization of Petroleum Exporting Countries.
I. Title.
HD9560.5.T527   1993
338.2'7282 — dc20
93-5826 CIP

Printed in the United States of America

1 2 3 4 5 97 96 95 94 93

Dedicated To
my wife Dawn and our daughters,
Elizabeth and Jessica

CONTENTS

INTRODUCTION

You don't have to be an economist to understand petroleum economics. And you certainly don't have to understand anything about petroleum economics to render an opinion on the subject.

In the 1970s we heard news reports about oil companies profiteering by not unloading and selling tanker loads of crude oil. The United States, the world's single largest consumer of petroleum products, adopted an energy policy founded on the assumption that the country and the world had all but exhausted their petroleum resource.

We grew smarter in the 1980s. No longer did we believe that something called Big Oil set the price of crude and, therefore, gasoline, diesel, heating oil, and other petroleum products. Now we blamed the Organization of Petroleum Exporting Countries. Price jumps following the Arab oil embargo of 1973 and the Iranian Revolution of 1979 taught us that OPEC, not the Seven Sisters, set prices, which at the beginning of the decade seemed certain to climb forever.

Somehow, though, OPEC missed a cue. Crude prices collapsed in 1986. One of the Seven Sisters disappeared. Another one went bankrupt.

Then came the 1990s and with them the wisdom that prices don't rise unless there's a shortage. If they do and nobody can find a shortage then something fishy must be afoot.

The test came in August 1990, when Iraqi troops invaded Kuwait. The Kuwaiti shutdown and retaliatory embargo of Iraqi exports removed 4.3 million B/D of crude and products from the international market. Prices shot up $12 or so to $30/bbl.

There must have been a shortage.

The International Energy Agency of Paris—probably the single best clearinghouse for basic international petroleum market data—didn't see things that way. The market had sustained its greatest shock in modern history, the overnight loss of 4.3 million B/D of internationally traded oil. Yet IEA saw no reason to implement the program of strategic inventory withdrawals and oil sharing it had been established to administer in the aftermath of the Arab embargo of the early 1970s. Diligent IEA officials looked high and low and could only ask, "Where's the shortage?"

So why did the crude price jump to $30 per barrel and more in late 1990? Were those infernal tankers waiting over the horizon again? Had the Seven—uh, Six—Sisters returned to curse consumers again?

Indeed, prices quickly retreated once Iraqi forces proved to have been fiercer in the advance press dispatches than they were in actual combat. With Saddam Hussein caged up in Baghdad, a complacent industrialized world could blithely conclude that there had been no shortage, after all, and could safely revert to its characteristic habits of suspecting the worst of the oil industry and burning cheap, if in some cases highly taxed, petroleum. Supplementing the theory that oil companies conspired to keep prices high came the widespread presumption that U.S. President George Bush and the Saudi royal family were in cahoots to keep prices low.

Throughout all of this generally confused period, global petroleum resources showed no sign whatever that they were anywhere near the point of exhaustion.

We seem not to know much about petroleum economics. We seem not to have arrived at a durable explanation for price movements, for OPEC behavior, or for consumer responses to changes in other market variables.

Yet the basics are not that difficult. Contrary to the assertions of many, oil behaves like any other commodity. When supply rises relative to demand, prices tend to sag. When demand rises relative to supply, prices tend to rise. What can be difficult, given petroleum's inevitable and distortive byproducts—politics and misinformation—is bringing the basics of supply, demand, and price into unrefracted focus and discerning the crucial trends and connections. That's what this book is about.

This book will not turn its readers into economists. Nor is it written for economists, who may nevertheless want to look over this layman's shoulder to see where he strays from professional orthodoxy. Be warned. He will.

This book is written by a noneconomist for noneconomists—oil industry technicians who want better to understand what is happening to their business, journalists and other observers, perhaps even those blessed people who read about things for the sheer joy of knowing to the extent possible what is going on in the world. For good or bad, it is indeed the case that what happens in the petroleum markets affects us all.

Because this book will attempt not to encroach upon territory best left to professionals (much), it will employ as little as possible the usual measuring, modeling, and predicting. That intention should not be construed as disapproval of those altogether right-eous pursuits. For we lay folk, they simply are not all that neces-sary. What we need to know is how to assess the photograph, not how to process the film.

What this book will do is show you how to observe the oil market; how to assess the broad forces influencing supply, demand, and price; and how to distinguish political smoke from economic flame. It will explain in undergraduate terms how the market works and define the principal measures of its not-so-mysterious comings and goings.

After you have finished reading you will know where to look for information about this most international of markets. You will know how to read and interpret the data. And you will be able at least to converse with professional economists and still respect yourself in the morning.

A final disclaimer: You will not learn here how accurately to predict oil prices. You will learn why it is best not to try. Petroleum economists understand the perils of forecasting oil prices, which is why they make other people pay them to do it and never guarantee their work. Let that be your first important lesson about petroleum economics. I hope you enjoy the rest.

CHAPTER ONE

A
CLOSED
SYSTEM

The law of supply and demand works.

It works even in the case of petroleum.

The law of supply and demand works in the case of petroleum despite government officials who think they know better than markets do what oil prices should be, despite groups of exporters bent on manipulating prices to their political wishes, despite a recurrent political attitude that says oil is too important to be left to the market's often murky fancies.

In the 1990s, the law of supply and demand works in the case of petroleum perhaps better than ever before. At least its workings are easier to keep track of than ever before.

Around the world, markets are in vogue. Former Warsaw Pact nations are trying out the rigors of capitalism. Countries are selling state commercial holdings in a healthy phenomenon known as privatization. And a decade or so of apparent surplus has kept oil

Oil means work, and not just for the people who find, produce, and process it. It is one of the world's most important forms of energy, which is essential to economic development, jobs, and human progress. The workers here are "tripping" pipe aboard a drilling vessel at work in Bruce condensate field in the U.K. North Sea. A "bit" at the bottom of the pipe cuts through rock below the seabottom to drill the well. Photo courtesy of British Petroleum Co. plc.

prices in check, suppressing government pretensions about dominating markets, at least in the industrialized world.

In the same period, oil markets have developed windows. Trading has matured in futures contracts and options, creating a reliable analog to the less visible markets for physical barrels of crude oil and petroleum products. Computers have made it possible to track physical transactions in near real time: Oil prices change moment by moment, and the information appears almost instantaneously on video screens around the world.

This is not to say that the law of supply and demand did not work before the 1990s, before the futures and options markets developed, before computers connected traders and speculators in all parts of the globe, before governments in the major consuming nations abdicated their vain attempts to manipulate markets. The law of supply and demand always works, which is to say that markets always work. When price information is slow, and when governments allocate supplies, dictate demand, and otherwise try to set oil prices, markets seem to work slowly and do work inefficiently. They work nevertheless.

Markets, for example, behaved with cruel rationality after the oil embargo of 1973–74. Yet the governments of major consuming nations responded to the embargo as though market forces had nothing to do with events. History shows how wrong they were.

The embargo was the work of Arab oil exporters, most of them members of the Organization of Petroleum Exporting Countries. The Arab countries curtailed crude oil exports to the United States and The Netherlands in response to those countries' support of Israel in the Yom Kippur War. The United States, by far the world's largest single oil market, reacted by keeping in force oil price controls adopted earlier as part of an anti-inflation program. Later, the country tried to allocate supplies on the basis of historic consumption.

The response was predictable; indeed, it had been predicted by observers who understood markets. Prices held below market levels by controls stimulated demand. Yet allocation rules withheld supplies. There was shortage in the sense that oil failed to appear where buyers willing to pay the market price needed it. And it came courtesy not of OPEC but of Washington, D.C., manifest in the infamous queues at gasoline service stations.

Market forces ultimately overwhelmed the artificial controls and mocked stated policy of the postembargo 1970s, which emphasized conservation. After falling in 1974 and 1975 in response to the initial price shocks resulting from the embargo, total demand for petroleum products rose in each of the next three years in the United States, finishing the period 9% higher than it had been in 1973 (Table 1–1).[1] The reason: domestic crude oil and selected product prices kept cheap by government mandate. That is precisely the response predicted by the law of supply and demand, and precisely the opposite of U.S. policy.

Sometimes, it seems, the law of supply and demand works only too well.

S MOKE
A ND
H AZE

f petroleum adheres so closely to the law of supply and demand, why do politicians, journalists, even oil industry representatives claim either that it is exempt from economic stricture or that market forces are too

TABLE 1-1
CONSUMPTION IN A
PRICE-CONTROLLED ENVIRONMENT

crude Year	U.S. petroleum products consumption (Million barrels)	World crude price* (Dollars per barrel)	U.S. price**
1970	5,364	1.80	3.18
1971	5,553	2.29	3.39
1972	5,990	2.59	3.39
1973	6,317	11.65	3.89
1974	6,078	11.25	6.87
1975	5,958	12.67	7.67
1976	6,391	13.00	8.19
1977	6,727	13.66	8.57
1978	6,879	14.34	9.00
1979	6,757	27.95	12.64
1980	6,242	32.00	21.59

*Saudi Arabia Light crude, estimated "posted price"
based on long term contract prices and spot market quotations.
**U.S. average crude oil price at the wellhead; price con-
trols in effect for some types through 1979.
Note: The difference between world and U.S. prices during the period of controls shows the extent to which the
government subsidized consumption. Product prices have
a more direct effect on consumption; some of them also
were limited by controls.
Source: *Energy Statistics Sourcebook*

whimsical for this most important of commodities? And why do
petroleum supply, demand, and price behave at times in seemingly
contrary ways?

The answer lies partly in the size and complexity of the global
oil market and partly in the international political maneuvering

that always plays some role in petroleum decision-making. An overhang of inventories, for example, can delay price reactions to an interruption in production from some important exporting country. OPEC meetings can seem more like contests of political hegemony than serious attempts to balance worldwide supply, demand, and price. Futures markets might respond wildly to a surprising change in U.S. gasoline inventories one week, then ignore an even greater change a few weeks later.

To the casual observer, it all can appear to be something quite different from rational market behavior. To observers attuned to the conspiracy incantations of uninformed politicians, it might even seem rigged.

What's more, even experts can be fooled. According to the guiding industry wisdom of the postembargo 1970s and early 1980s, oil prices (thanks to steady depletion of the petroleum resource) would climb forever. The lesson of that period is that any presumption about petroleum's immunity to the law of supply and demand eventually will be proven wrong.

Petroleum just seems immune to economic law at times because data have not caught up with market responses, because political theatrics have drawn attention away from market mechanics, or because governments have erected smokescreens such as price controls or consumption limits.

Fast as information travels in a computerized market, it takes time for reporting services to make sense of the huge volume of data generated every hour, day, week, and month. Petroleum statistics mongers know better than to assume that one week's change of direction in prices or demand constitutes a trend. The market adjusts to changes in its key forces immediately, but it may take several weeks for the change to become evident in the statistics watched by trained observers.

Watching
The
Elephant
Shift

I t is an enormous market, an enormous industry. The very magnitude of the numbers that the market generates can be perplexing. Just the units of measurement themselves can confuse beginners.

The basic unit of petroleum industry measurement is the barrel, a measure of petroleum volume equal to 42 U.S. gallons. It is simply a unit of measure, not the description of a container in common use anywhere within the industry. In many parts of the world, industry operating rates are denominated in metric tons, or tonnes, which of course measure weight instead of volume. On average, a tonne amounts to about 7.3 barrels (bbl), although specific crudes vary from the average due to differences in density. In the United States, the volumetric barrel measurement is used almost exclusively. Elsewhere, petroleum amounts are often measured in tonnes. In the market, however, prices are most commonly quoted on a per-barrel basis. For that reason, this book will measure petroleum amounts in barrels.

So how big is the market? In 1991, the world consumed 65.5 million bbl of petroleum products every day. Production, the amount of oil and natural gas liquids extracted from the ground through wells, averaged 64.2 million barrels per day (B/D). On average, 32.3 million B/D of crude oil and petroleum products moved in international trade. At the end of 1991, proved reserves—the amount of crude oil known to lie underground and to be economically recoverable with current technology—totaled an estimated 1 trillion bbl.[2] These are not trivial numbers.

The totals and averages agglomerate national production figures from no fewer than 85 countries with producing reserves and consumption data from every country in the world. Other crucial market data come from major refining centers such as Rotterdam, Singapore, and the U.S. Gulf Coast. The important numbers are not just large and varied, then, but also geographically dispersed by source. Computers and instantaneous communications notwithstanding, the petroleum market is in many ways an elephant: quick to react but often slow to make a show of it.

Size has a corrective effect on extra-market influences. It is by no means the case that the market functions without interference in all places. Some Third World oil-producing countries palliate their electorates by subsidizing fuel prices. More to the point, OPEC members, individually or in groups, occasionally propose to raise or lower crude oil prices for reasons that have more to do with politics than economics. The Arab embargo mentioned earlier established a legacy that probably will outlive OPEC.

Yet the market always prevails. It certainly did so after the embargo. Just as market forces ultimately crushed U.S. efforts to limit prices and consumption, they vanquished OPEC fantasies about controlling global politics by manipulating oil prices and, therefore, economies. It just took a while for the elephant's new posture to become apparent.

Again, a glance at historical data shows what happened. Worldwide demand for crude oil followed the U.S. pattern after the embargo: two years of decline in response to the shock of withheld exports and higher prices, followed by several years of steady gains—four worldwide vs. three in the United States alone. But the market received another jolt in 1978. Iran's Islamic Revolution halted the country's oil production of nearly 6 million B/D. Crude prices quickly quadrupled. OPEC spent the next five years trying in vain to hold prices at the elevated levels.

Consumers had other ideas. Product prices based on $34/bbl crude encouraged conservation. Consumption began to fall in 1978 in the United States and in 1979 worldwide. It kept falling until the mid-1980s and did not climb back to peak levels until 1988 worldwide. In the United States, demand for crude oil at this writing had never reattained 1978's peak annual average of 18.3 million B/D.

How did this demand adjustment affect OPEC? It forced the exporters' group into a wholesale change of strategy. At a fateful meeting in March 1983, OPEC tried to cut its members' total production in an effort to defend a target crude price set $5/bbl below its unachievable predecessor. Technically, it was OPEC's first effort to function as a true cartel, to limit supply in order to support price. Before, OPEC had been following a market in transition, not controlling it as so often is alleged.

OPEC's effort to perform as a cartel didn't work. The group couldn't defend the $29/bbl target price it set in 1983. It tried further production cuts but could not sustain the discipline necessary to collectively limit supply. By 1985, Saudi Arabia, the group's biggest producer, had had enough. It had cut production to the bone. It had seen demand reduced by past price run-ups. And it had witnessed a classic supply response: development of new sources of crude oil and alternatives that had not been economic when oil fetched $3—or even $12—per barrel.

In September 1985, therefore, the Saudis began to produce and sell oil at will, destroying prices and OPEC's untenable aspirations for them. A strategy of price control gave way to a more realistic one oriented to market share. The world has not been the same since.

To repeat, the petroleum market works. Thanks to occasional intrusions by the governments of producing and consuming nations, the market's workings may not always be quickly evident; they may even seem perverse. The market works nevertheless.

Ask the authors of failed energy strategies in the United States, the United Kingdom, and other high-demand countries that have tried in vain to insulate their consumers from price changes.

Ask OPEC.

Ask a rapidly contracting worldwide oil industry.

They all will attest that the petroleum market really works.

It always has.

It always will.

A
COMPLEX
SYSTEM

The challenge for anyone wanting to make sense of this giant business is (1) to waft aside the political smoke so often aswirl in a market change and (2) to assemble short-term signals from various market segments in order to recognize the important forces at work and to determine what they mean.

It is not always easy. Every Wednesday in the United States, for example, prices of oil futures contracts on the New York Mercantile Exchange rise or fall in response to basic industry data released by the American Petroleum Institute after trading the day before. Can a market observer tell much from these price changes?

Usually, no. In fact, the data on which each Wednesday's price changes are based usually are revised later. By then, of course, traders are basing their buying and selling decisions on an altogether different set of statistics. The price flutters characteristic of a given trading day usually mean little to the casual observer. Trends that show evidence of durability are what are most important to meaningful market assessment.

Daily oil price changes seldom signal much important in the way of fundamental market change—except, of course, to traders. To be sure, oil company traders of physical crude oil and products, as well as decision-makers for refining and marketing operations, keep a close eye on the prices of futures and, increasingly, options contracts. Provision of such a window on the market is one of futures trading's vital functions.

But an observer wanting to understand basic market forces and to assess their meanings for the future must take a broader view. The way to do that is to look at the vast, complex petroleum market as a single system of containment. The market is, in fact, a closed system.

PHYSICAL CONSTRAINTS

From the wellhead to the point of consumption, oil is subject to physical constraint.

What we call an oil field is really an underground layer of rock. It contains a finite volume of fluid hydrocarbon. The amount of oil and gas this rock ultimately surrenders and the rate at which it does so depend on a variety of factors, some natural, some not. The natural factors include the nature of the rock itself: how readily fluids pass through it, what natural pressures exist within it, how much oil it contains. Unnatural factors include the number of wells drilled into the rock, the efficiencies with which the wells enable fluids to escape the rock and pass into what's called production tubing, size of that tubing, and the amount and efficiency of surface equipment installed to enhance production and recovery rates. Obviously, the amount and efficiency of all this equipment depend upon the amount of money invested in it. That amount of money depends upon what some investor expects in the way of oil volumes, production rates, and future oil prices. Similarly, the rates at which production equipment is operated depend upon current prices.

In just this first, relatively short step that petroleum takes toward the market—from its natural underground habitat to the Earth's surface—there are constraints; namely, equipment and money.

And what happens next? Usually, produced fluids have to pass through equipment that separates natural gases from the liquids, which can contain salt water and condensates as well as crude oil. These must be separated by equipment that has operating limits. The crude may have to be stored in tanks with only so much volume, where it will be picked up by a tank truck. Or it may move into a pipeline through which only so much crude can travel in a given time.

Whether it moves by truck or pipeline or both, crude must pass through the refining process, which turns it into useful petroleum products. At various stages, it usually spends time in more tanks with finite volumes. And its chemical transformations occur in refinery equipment that, like pipelines, can operate only up to certain limits.

Finished petroleum products then must move to consumers, following journeys that can involve more pipelines, more trucks, and more tanks, all with their own carrying limits. Even the gasoline pump, the most visible piece of equipment in this complicated process, can dispense only so much product at a time.

It is a system of constraints: metal tubes and cylinders that extract petroleum from the ground, move it from place to place, and rearrange its molecules. And the system has definite limits called capacities: production capacities, pipeline throughput capacities, refining capacities, and storage capacities. These capacities, in turn, depend upon the amount of money invested in them—in other words, capital, the supply of which has limits of its own.

At any given time the system operates at some percentage of its total ability to produce, process, store, transport, and sell petroleum. But the system is always closed: physically, because if it were not there would be a nasty mess somewhere, and economically, because its capacities have limits that depend upon the collective decisions of people with money to invest.

SHORTAGE
AND
SURPLUS

his all may seem self-evident, but the implications are not. The notion of the petroleum market as a closed, however complicated, system has enormous consequences for what we often describe as "shortage" and "surplus."

What is oil shortage? A popular definition probably would run something like this: a noticeable absence of oil at some point of would-be consumption.

What is oil surplus? The answer to this one might be: the existence of too much oil at the point of consumption or elsewhere along the distribution system.

That these are the popular and, in many places, official understandings of the terms is in many ways apparent. During the 1990–91 Iraqi occupation of Kuwait, the most threatening interruption to oil supplies since the International Energy Agency established its emergency oil sharing system, officials in many countries and in the IEA itself kept citing an absence of apparent shortage as a reason not to make use of emergency oil supplies. They treated shortage as something discernible, as a measurable absence of supply. They found none, of course. Absences cannot be measured.

The question that must be asked about this approach is this: How would one recognize a measurable absence of supply if, indeed, such a thing ever existed?

The popular view of surplus is so common it has become a cliché: The world is awash in oil. It is as though surplus meant supply exceeding the closed system's capacity for containing it.

Well, the world never has been awash in oil and probably never will be so. If the world were awash in oil of sufficient volatility, the consequences of smoking in nondesignated areas would certainly be more severe than they are at present.

It is a closed system. If measurable absences indeed could occur, the system would collapse. And if physical surpluses, in the sense of supplies exceeding the system's capacity, could occur, there would be a perpetual spill somewhere in the world.

BETTER
DEFINITIONS

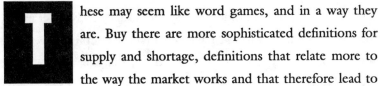

T hese may seem like word games, and in a way they are. Buy there are more sophisticated definitions for supply and shortage, definitions that relate more to the way the market works and that therefore lead to more precise assessments of market behavior. The key is to think about the market as the closed system that it is.

As we shall discuss in more detail later, the crucial market forces of supply, demand, and price constantly influence, and are influenced by, one another. The market constantly seeks a balance of forces that economists call "equilibrium." A significant change in one of these forces creates adjustments in the others until the market reattains equilibrium. Equilibrium exists mainly in theory; in reality, it exists fleetingly, if ever. The fickle nature of equilibrium need not concern us now. What is important is the market's irrepressible yearning for it.

So long as there is oil that can be extracted from the ground, the pressures of supply, demand, and price in the direction of equilibrium ensure that there can be no shortage in the sense of a measurable absence. Exceptions to this rule result from government intrusions, such as the U.S. allocation regulations mentioned earlier, that prevent oil's moving to the consumers that most need it. Otherwise, when a significant amount of oil vanishes from the market for whatever reason, prices rise as buyers compete for replacement volumes from the supplies that remain. In response to the consequently higher prices, consumers with the least intense need for oil find ways to do without it. Demand falls. The market balances at some point characterized by lower volumes and higher prices than before.

Similarly, there are times when the petroleum market can deliver more oil than consumers collectively need. This, in fact, is the market's normal condition; the system usually can deliver more than is needed. A normal, balanced market contains a certain amount of capacity that can be utilized but that will not be until prices climb.

For the sake of example, let us say the market is in relative balance operating at X% of maximum capacity with prices at Y dollars per barrel. And let us assume that economic activity declines. This normally reduces oil demand. Now, therefore, the market must contract. Its capacity utilization rate must fall to less than X% of the maximum system-wide operating rate. Why? Because at some point all storage will be full, and the alternative to reducing capacity utilization of the closed system is to spill oil onto the ground or into the sea. And that seldom happens except by accident.

Someone must quit producing, processing, transporting, and selling petroleum in such a case. And the mechanism of price determines who makes the sacrifice. When the system can deliver more oil than consumers need, prices fall as sellers compete for buyers. Eventually, prices drop to the point that some sellers (and producers and refiners and pipeline operators) cannot make money at the going price, so they idle capacity under their control. This, then, is surplus, and if everyone has been careful, not a drop has been spilled.

To be sure, these are broad, theoretical explanations of how the market works. In reality, it is never easy to observe these phenomena as they occur. If we were discussing the internal combustion engine instead of the petroleum market, we would be at the point of saying that controlled explosions make pistons go up and down, which in turn make crankshafts go around. It will be the function of later chapters to discuss the market equivalents of carburetion, compression, ignition, and so forth.

But it is not too early to provide functional definitions of shortage and surplus:

Shortage is a condition of the market in which demand is constrained by limits in supply.

Surplus is a condition of the market in which supply is con-

strained by limits in demand.

No measurable absences. No worlds awash in oil.

In freely operating markets, those measurable absences and deliberate spills never occur. What do occur are shifts in two forces (demand and price or supply and price) large enough to effect a constraint on the third.

A principal function of petroleum economics is to identify, even to anticipate, conditions of supply or demand constraint—in other words, to predict shortage and surplus. Petroleum economics even can detect the more-common subtle movements toward or away from these conditions of constraint, a function essential to predicting changes in price.

Economists have computers and databases and graduate degrees and econometric models and a whole profession's worth of skills and knowledge to help them turn mountains of real-world data into meaningful assessments of market change. Casual observers have only the commonly published oil industry statistics, of which they may or may not be able to make sense.

The tricks are to ask the right questions and to know where to look for the answers.

The right questions are these:

1. How much oil does the world need?

2. How much oil can (or will) the world deliver to market?

3. How will prices interact with answers to questions 1 and 2?

The rest of this book will deal with those questions and with using available sources of information to find their answers.

REFERENCES

1. *Energy Statistics Sourcebook, Oil & Gas Journal* Energy Database, PennWell Books, 1990.

2. *BP Statistical Review of World Energy,* British Petroleum Co. plc, June 1992.

CHAPTER TWO

CONSUMER
POWER

According to Chapter 1, the first basic question of petroleum market analysis is this: How much oil does the world need? The answer comes from consumers.

In the 1970s and 1980s, it was politically fashionable to regard the consumer as a powerless victim of nefarious forces conspiring to raise prices forever. Market analysis in this view became a morality play: Big oil companies and Arab sheiks conspiring to exploit consumers, who were understood to need oil products so badly that they would pay whatever prices the conspirators forced upon them. Policies emanating from this view incorporated price controls, conservation mandates, and subsidization of uneconomic, nonpetroleum fuels.

As it happens, consumers are not such meek wretches, after all. They reduce their consumption when oil products become too expensive. Consuming-nation governments, in fact, have never found a way to retaliate against the alleged mischief of Big Oil and OPEC that is more effective than what consumers, acting on their

Consumers answer the basic question about how much oil the world needs. The petroleum industry responds by installing the equipment, such as pipelines, needed to deliver oil products to where they are needed.

own in pursuit of their own interests, do in response to price increases: consume less than before. Oil companies, whether they're owned by private investors or the royal families of desert sheikdoms, exist to make money selling oil. When they cannot sell oil because their prices are too high, they know exactly what to do.

The intrusions of government only interfere with these altogether righteous processes. We have seen that U.S. market manipulations after the Arab oil embargo worked against themselves—stimulating consumption, creating physical shortages by keeping plentiful oil away from where it was needed, and ultimately failing to restrain prices. It's important also to understand how these manipulations produced such perversion. Chapter 1 introduced the concept of demand response to changing price. This chapter will examine demand responses in more detail and from several perspectives, will show how the responses became distorted during the period of price controls, and will introduce several economic principles and measures crucial to accurate assessment of oil demand.

CONSUMER DECISION-MAKING

il consumers base their decisions about whether to purchase oil and from whom to purchase it on these parameters:

1. How much money they have.

2. How much oil costs.

3. The intensity of their need for oil.

Obviously, individual consumers function within these parameters in a wide variety of ways. Consider three hypothetical consumers and their responses to a market change.

Stanley, third-generation owner of a commodities brokerage firm, plans a trip to the islands aboard his 50-ft yacht.

Richard, a middle-aged computer programmer who commutes from the suburbs, is trying to save money for his three children's educations but hopes to work in a late-summer vacation in the mountains.

Allen lives in an apartment and works in a toy factory downtown, fitting rubber pads onto pogo-stick footpieces. Life has been a mighty struggle for Allen ever since his wife ran away with the apartment building's maintenance man after running up the credit card balances.

Let us assume that a hurricane strikes the nearest refining center, forcing operations to cease. The interruption in supplies causes oil product prices to rise by, say, 10%. How do our consumers react?

The most obvious response comes from Allen, who no longer can afford to buy gasoline for his old Chevrolet and now must ride the bus to work. The gasoline market has lost a consumer—a consumer who lives at what economists call the margin of demand.

Richard can still afford to drive to work. Now, however, he must choose between the trip to the mountains and the savings deposit he planned to make against his oldest child's college tuition.

For Stanley, unlike Richard, a 10% increase in the price of oil products is no reason to cancel vacation plans. But it might be reason to drive his BMW to the marina instead of flying the helicopter.

The economic notion of demand is nothing more than the grand total of decisions such as these.

THE ECONOMY'S ROLE

llen, Richard, and Stanley have demonstrated how price affects demand when it rises. The reverse should be obvious: If oil prices drop by 10%, Allen does not need to switch to the bus, Richard might plan a side trip once he reaches the mountains, and Stanley does not think twice about flying to the marina. The grand total of decisions such as these amount to a demand increase.

Price, however, does not work solo as an influence on oil demand. One of the parameters in consumer decision-making, after all, is the amount of money consumers bring to bear on their decisions.

In the example, we examined the different effects a sudden oil price rise might have on three hypothetical consumers in three very different circumstances of income. The point there was to compare their responses to the price jump.

Let us assume now, however, that these three oil consumers work in a booming economy and that, further, the day before the oil price jump each received a raise in salary. If those raises each amounted to more than 10%—the assumed size of the oil price rise—then none of our consumers would feel nearly the pressure to adjust behavior that he felt earlier.

What if the reverse were true? Let us assume now that the economy is slumping, that Richard and Allen have received layoff notices, and that Stanley's firm has reported its first loss in history.

This might be enough to persuade Stanley to cancel his yacht trip; now he burns gasoline traveling to the boat dealer to put the craft up for sale. Richard cancels the mountain trip but uses the automobile traveling to job interviews. Poor Allen leaves his Chevy in the apartment parking lot and walks the streets, seeking work and avoiding phone calls from the credit card companies. Now economic doldrums amplify demand responses to a price jump.

The economic background against which a price change occurs is crucial to the degree of demand response.

Moreover, economic growth or contraction influences demand even if oil price remain constant. Again, let's examine our friends in the circumstance of a changing economy without the shock of a price jump. Now times are good, Allen and Richard are working, and each has recently received a 12% pay increase. Stanley's firm is flourishing, so his salary and dividend income has just jumped by 12% as well.

Now Stanley begins thinking about an extra week in the islands. Richard starts to wonder whether renting a recreational vehicle would make the mountain trip more fun than it would be if he just drove the station wagon. Allen catches up on his credit card payments and begins looking at second-hand bass boats. The consequence of each potential decision here involves rising oil consumption.

When people have more money to spend—when, that is, the economy in which they live and work is healthy—they usually spend some portion of it on extra activities that require oil.

The reverse case is simple to imagine: recession, salary cuts or job losses, canceled plans for recreation, more attention to savings—including on costs of oil. Economic health strongly influences individual oil consumption decisions and, therefore, overall petroleum demand.

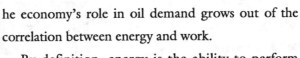

Energy Consumption And Work

The economy's role in oil demand grows out of the correlation between energy and work.

By definition, energy is the ability to perform work. Also by definition, more work is performed in a robust economy than in a feeble one. All else being equal, therefore, an economy consumes more energy in periods of growth (high work levels) than in periods of stagnation (low work levels). Some significant share of that energy always will be petroleum.

"Work" in this context means human activity of all kinds, including play: Stanley's yacht trip, Richard's mountain vacation, Allen's bass boat. In economic terms, one person's play means work for someone else. And work means income.

Consider an isolated economy: the toy factory that employs Allen. In a period of moderate demand for pogo sticks, factory profits may be sufficient to keep all workers employed but not all equipment in operation at maximum rates. The people are working; they're just not making as many pogo sticks as they would be if demand were greater. It is easy to see that energy use declines slightly because factory equipment is not running at full tilt. But it is not as though there had been a 50% layoff, which would have meant half the number of workers driving automobiles to work. In microcosm, the energy demand effects of an economic slowdown seem slight.

But the workers under these conditions do not receive the same bonuses and wage increases that they would if demand for pogo sticks were stronger. The factory's owners do not make as much money. Total incomes generated by the factory—wages and salaries to the employees and profits to the owners—are not as great as they would be in better times.

In good times, the factory's workers and owners have more money to spend and to save. When they spend it they boost demand for someone else's products. And, in economic terms, it doesn't matter whether they spend for fun or necessity. When the happy employees and owners of our busy toy factory buy food, they contribute to demand for farm products and thereby stimulate agricultural activity. When they buy jet skis they augment the profits and wage-paying capacity of factories that make jet skis and fishing reels.

What if they save the money instead? Unless they bury the booty in a jar, they still boost economic activity. Banks lend against their deposits; the more deposits they have, the more money they can lend for things like factory expansions and new farms.

Economic phenomena thus do not occur in isolation. There are always ripple effects. Work means income. More income means more work. And more work requires more energy, which means rising demand for oil and other fuels.

Price, then, exerts a strong influence on oil demand. But it must be assessed in the context of economic conditions. When people make fuel purchase decisions they look at not just price but also at their ability to pay. Individually, that ability depends on income. And collective income depends on economic conditions.

THE
MARGINAL
CONSUMER
AND
ELASTICITIES

Fuel choices have one other basic parameter: the intensity of need.

Fuel consumers decide whether to buy or not to buy on the basis of fuel price, their abilities to pay, and how badly they need the product. When fuel prices rise faster than incomes—that is, faster than consumers' abilities to pay—the number of decisions not to buy increases. This is a very uneven process. Often, consumers are barely conscious of it.

This chapter earlier referred to consumer Allen's residing at the "margin of demand." That means an extra unit of gasoline price—a penny per gallon somewhere in that 10% increase—caused a change in Allen's consumption behavior: He quit driving to work. He represents the marginal consumer at that price.

Economists use the term "margin" in a variety of contexts. It always has to do with the idea of something extra. If gasoline prices gain an extra nickel per gallon, what happens to demand? Theoretically, at every level of gasoline price, there are consumers paying absolutely as much as they can afford, so that if prices rise by any amount they will have to reduce consumption. Those consumers are said to be at the margin of consumption at the price just before the increase that made them change behavior.

The notion of margin is just that: a notion. Complexities of human nature and disparities of circumstance make it impossible to measure or predict behavior at the margin with much accuracy. But the idea of economic margin helps us to understand the workings of the market. As gasoline prices rise they pass through a spectrum of consumption margins in a process that reduces demand to some degree. Economic torpor amplifies the effect—it lowers the price-consumption margins of consumers—because it reduces fuel buyers' abilities to pay and their intensities of need.

This phenomenon is less a product of economic class distinction than it might appear to be. Even the wealthy reside at some price-consumption margin. Remember Stanley? A 10% price increase for oil products didn't deter him from taking his yacht trip or driving to the marina. He didn't reside at the price-consumption margin for marine fuel or gasoline in the price spectrum covered in the 10% increase. But he was a marginal consumer for aviation fuel. Joy riding in helicopters is expensive business, even for the wealthy.

Related to this notion of margin is what economists call elasticities. This simply refers to the amount by which one market variable changes in response to a change in another. A price rise tends to discourage consumption. Demand thus is elastic with respect to price. Supply, as we will see later, is elastic with respect to price as well. Economists try to measure elasticities. Some even feel obliged to prove that they exist. There are times, after all, when demand growth seems undeterred by a price rise— when, in other words, demand seems inelastic with respect to price. But there's always an explanation. The demand growth may result from a booming economy, so incomes are rising faster than oil prices. At such a time demand indeed seems inelastic. A relevant question, however, is what demand would have been in such an economy if prices had not risen. It probably would have been greater, although no one can prove it.

According to one very interesting theory, oil demand elasticity is greater when prices rise suddenly than when they ease up by the same amount over a period of months or years. A gradual price increase gives consumers time to make careful decisions, while a price jolt forces them into immediate changes of behavior. Market purists tend to believe that price rises of equal size have more or less equal demand consequences whether they occur immediately or over a stretch of time. The demand responses simply get camouflaged by intervening economic and market phenomena in the case of gradual price growth. The purpose here is not to take sides in an issue that rightly belongs in the arena of economics professionals; rather, it is to arm nonprofessional observers with one more dimension with which to examine the behavior of petroleum markets.

A
LOOK
BACK

he world learned important lessons about prices and oil consumption during the decade of the 1970s.

Crude oil prices jumped by 255% between 1973 and 1974 in response to the Arab oil embargo. And worldwide demand for crude oil, which had been climbing steadily in the preceding years, took an immediate drop of 2%.

Things became muddled in the following years. By 1976 demand was rising again, even though prices remained nearly four times their pre-embargo levels. How could this be?

There are three explanations. One is a surge in economic activity after the slump that followed the price jolt in 1973–74. Much of the activity resulted from investments by the oil-exporting countries that suddenly became wealthy from the price jump. This was the famous "recycling of petrodollars."

In addition, many countries tried to cushion their economies from the oil price shock by putting more units of currency into circulation—literally creating money. Unfortunately, economic productivity did not keep pace. The result was inflation, which in retrospect makes price levels of the middle and late 1970s somewhat illusory. The prices quoted here are nominal (uncorrected for inflation) rather than real (corrected for inflation). Chapter 4 covers inflation in more detail.

The third explanation for the muddled demand response of the mid-1970s is that the governments of major consuming nations, the United States in particular, set limits on prices to protect consumers. It is worth taking a closer look at the distortions created by the period of U.S. price controls because it illustrates demand responses so well.

When a government sets artificial limits on prices of an internationally traded product or commodity, its foreign suppliers divert some part of their exports to countries where they can sell at greater prices. So external supply available to the country imposing controls diminishes.

Furthermore, with prices unable to rise, the reality of diminished supply cannot become apparent to consumers as it should: by way of price. The hypothetical consumers from earlier in this chapter show what happens.

Let's assume again that a hurricane disrupts oil supply. Let's also assume that the government freezes prices of crude oil and petroleum products at precrisis levels and sets in motion an allocation scheme aimed at limiting demand as well. Poor Allen does not switch to the bus because gasoline prices are controlled. Richard proceeds to the mountains and makes his tuition deposit as well. Stanley cranks up the helicopter and makes a low pass over a garden party he couldn't make at the Bigelow mansion, for appearances' sake, then zooms off to the marina. Consumers, in other words, have no reason to change behavior because prices, subject as they are to government controls, do not change.

Things seem splendid for everyone involved—for a while. But consider the pressures here: Supply, already limited by the hurricane, has come under further constraint due to the reluctance of exporters to sell into a market with capped prices. Demand nevertheless remains free to grow because prices, now fixed by government decree, cannot discourage consumption as they otherwise should.

Demand grows while supply stalls. Supply functions as a constraint on demand—our definition of "shortage" from Chapter 1. At some point, consumers willing to pay the legal price cannot find anyone willing to sell at that level. When Stanley returns from the islands he can't refuel the chopper because aviation fuel is being rationed. Richard gets stuck in Piney Peak because the town's lone service station has exhausted its allocation by the time he arrives.

Allen's pay is docked by an hour because he has to wait in line to fill the Chevy.

Whatever the inconveniences suffered by Stanley, Richard, and Allen, there is no shortage in the sense of a physical absence of petroleum. Internationally, the system remains full of petroleum; it just takes a detour around markets with governments trying to immunize consumers from natural economic forces.

This is precisely what happened in the United States after 1973–74. Allocation programs, by which the government apportioned supply based on historic demand patterns, distorted the market even further. It was a fool's paradise: demand stimulated by low prices colliding with artificial consumption constraints, all happening in a period of lower supply. It was an economically untenable situation, and it did not last long. The United States began phasing out price controls in mid-1979.

By then, the next price jolt was under way. Islamic revolutionaries had overthrown the Shah of Iran. Exports all but ceased from a country that had been producing nearly 6 million B/D. Oil markets, sensitive since the Arab embargo to supply interruptions of this type, reacted wildly. Prices shot up. Although the effect wasn't as pronounced, Iran's invasion of Iraq in 1980 kept concerns about Middle East oil supplies high.

By 1980, however, price controls had vanished in the United States. Markets were freer to adjust to the latest disruption of supply than they had been to that of the Arab embargo. And adjust they did. From their 1978 level to their peak in 1982, oil prices increased by 168%. From a period peak in 1979, demand for crude oil worldwide fell by 10% by 1983 before resuming its climb. Prices shot up, and demand dropped significantly. Oil producers have felt the effect ever since. With prices free, consumers reacted quickly to the price run-up. Prices have not been that high ever since.

THE CONSERVATION CONTEST

he price jumps of 1973–74 and 1979–80 made energy conservation both a political ideal and a good economic deal. In the political arena, however, the subject often gets pummeled into meaninglessness.

A crude political ethic has emerged: Consumption of energy and especially of petroleum is bad; conservation means anything that reduces consumption in absolute terms and is, therefore, good. The ethic has taken on an environmentalist dimension under the assumption that oil combustion causes or aggravates global warming and other alleged planetary threats. The political momentum is nearly irresistible.

This climate has produced something of a contest of national energy and oil consumption figures. By every measure, the United States loses. It uses the most energy in terms of total consumption. In oil products alone, it accounted for one-fourth of total worldwide consumption in 1991.[1] It uses the most energy per capita (per person). It ranks among the highest in energy use per increment of economic growth.

The usual conclusion is that the United States leads the world in its energy wastefulness. It has become a litany. Here is but one example, from a business columnist in Houston: "We in the

United States waste terrific amounts of energy. Compared with Japan, it takes us twice as much energy to produce the same amount of goods or services."[2]

That analysis overlooks much—too much. For example, the U.S. consumption totals include fuels required to maintain the world's most powerful military force. By comparison, Japan's military fuel needs are negligible. The point here is not to argue whether the United States should or should not function as the world's military police force or whether Japan should play a larger role. The point is that the United States has adopted its role and expends the energy to carry it out; Japan has chosen the reverse. The energy consequences show up in the comparative energy consumption data.

Furthermore, the United States has 25 times the surface area of Japan. And United States citizens are very mobile. By virtue of the size of their country alone, they always have used—and always will use—significant amounts of transportation fuel. Partly for the same reasons, they drive vehicles larger than their counterparts in countries where overland travel is not so important a part of the culture.

Is it a waste of energy for a Houston resident to drive to St. Louis to visit parents and sibling, as this author does once a year or so? In many countries, driving distances of that magnitude (800 mi) do not exist. Was it a waste of energy for the United States to mount one of the largest military mobilizations in history to drive Iraqi invaders from Kuwait?

As are so many issues of international scale, energy consumption is relative to many considerations.

Comparing one country's oil consumption patterns with those of others is a complex exercise that generates too many facile conclusions. Countries vary in too many ways. The geographic size and military comparisons cited above for the United States and Japan are just two of them.

Degree of economic development is another—and an extremely important—one. Per capita energy consumption averages in advanced, industrialized countries significantly exceed those of countries with subsistence economies. To adhere to the popular ethic about oil consumption, this would mean industrialized countries must revert to the agrarian lifestyles of yesteryear. Such a step backward no doubt appeals to some segments of the modern population, but the aspiration is not realistic.

THE
ROLE
OF
TAXES

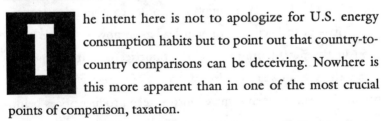

he intent here is not to apologize for U.S. energy consumption habits but to point out that country-to-country comparisons can be deceiving. Nowhere is this more apparent than in one of the most crucial points of comparison, taxation.

Consumption taxes on petroleum products essentially increase the prices of those products. They are not the economic equivalents of higher prices, because governments do different things with their receipts than private companies do. To consumers deciding whether to buy fuel, however, it matters little where the money goes. At the point of consumption, an increase in fuel tax amounts to an increase in price.

Petroleum product taxes vary greatly throughout the world. The reasons for imposing the taxes vary nearly as much. Countries that provide their citizens lavish services and benefits need revenue more than countries that do not; they are likely to tax petroleum consumption heavily because of their steep needs for funds. Countries with sophisticated highway networks often tax petroleum products as a way to finance road construction and maintenance. Some countries tax one fuel more than others in order to favor consumption of one over another. And, increasingly, countries raise taxes on oil simply to discourage consumption.

Among the world's economic leaders, the United States earns prominence for its generosity to consumers. At the middle of 1992, its taxes on gasoline averaged 9¢ per liter (l). Next lowest was Japan at 46¢/l. Italy ranked highest at 96¢/l. Others included France, 76¢/l; Germany, 70¢/l; Spain, 67¢/l; and the United Kingdom, 66¢/l (Table 2–1).[3]

Elsewhere, the reverse is often the case. Many developing countries subsidize oil consumption in order to stimulate economic activity—or to keep government leaders in power. This is common in the petroleum-producing countries of Latin America, where the subsidies are funded by profits of state-owned oil companies. The subsidies in some countries keep product prices below the cost of production, a practice that ultimately pushes state-owned oil companies toward insolvency.

Obviously, tax disparities such as these lead to uneven oil consumption patterns and create international frictions. There have been pressures, domestic and international, for the United States to raise its gasoline taxes. Similarly, the privatization movement of

TABLE 2–1
HOW OIL PRICES INFLUENCE CONSUMPTION*

Year	Price (Dollars per barrel)	Consumption (Thousand barrels per day)
1969	1.801	42,775
1970	1.80	46,415
1971	2.29	49,130
1972	2.59	52,735
1973	3.06	57,010
1974	10.89	56,360
1975	10.72	55,680
1976	11.51	59,120
1977	12.40	61,180
1978	12.70	63,095
1979	15.97	64,510
1980	28.00	62,125
1981	32.50	60,270
1982	34.00	58,410
1983	30.25	58,060
1984	29.00	59,015
1985	28.25	59,115
1986	18.06	60,775
1987	17.18	61,840
1988	14.36	63,565
1989	15.95	64,735

*Total world average annual crude oil consumption. Prices for Arabian Light crude oil, average government selling price except yearend posted prices for 1969–72.

Source: *Energy Statistics Sourcebook*, 1990, PennWell.

the 1980s and 1990s—in which countries sold their holdings in state-run oil and other companies—resulted greatly from the realization that countries cannot absorb indefinitely the costs associated with the inefficiencies of subsidization.

These issues can and should be argued in detail in the proper forums. This is not one of them. A reminder, however, is in order: Comparing one country's oil taxes with another's is as hazardous as comparing consumption patterns. The simple conclusion is usually wrong because the numbers do not tell the whole story.

MEASURING CONSERVATION

International comparisons of oil and energy consumption thus are fraught with peril. Countries and economies differ in too many significant ways. If those differences are not made part of the analysis, conclusions can be ridiculous. It generally is more meaningful to examine a single country's consumption patterns in terms of its own circumstances. But in that realm, too, there are difficulties.

Often, the righteous modern emphasis on conservation is corrupted by the notion that "conservation" means only "consuming less." Yet as this chapter has shown, consumption implies work (even when it involves play). An economy consumes more energy when it is active, when much work is being performed within it, than when it is not, there being no extraordinary conditions of price or supply. In the strict sense of consuming less, an economy can make impressive energy conservation gains by working less, that is, by forgoing economic growth. A far too infrequently asked question is: Is it worth it? Conservation in the form of mandatory reductions in energy consumption can be a very recessionary pursuit.

Conservation becomes more meaningful when energy (or petroleum) consumption is expressed in relation to economic activity. Then we can ask whether it is possible to use fewer barrels of oil, or tons of coal, or megawatts of electric power, without sacrificing work. If it is possible, and if we reduce energy consumption relative to economic growth, we become more efficient. This is a proper goal of government and business policy. It means infinitely more than simply consuming less.

What is more, energy use efficiency is imminently measurable. Governments measure economic activity in units, usually U.S. dollars, of gross national product (GNP) or gross domestic product (GDP). Both essentially measure an economy's total output of goods and services. And, as we have seen, governments also record total consumption of petroleum, coal, and other forms of energy.

The energy efficiency analysis asks this: How much energy does a country require to produce a unit of economic growth? Here we will examine both total energy consumption and petroleum consumption for three countries: the United States (a mature, robust economy half-dependent on imported oil), Japan (a mature, robust economy fully dependent on imported oil), and Thailand (a rapidly developing economy with rapidly growing energy needs).

ENERGY
EQUIVALENCY
CONVERSIONS

F irst, however, we must solve the problem of measuring total energy consumption. We cannot add barrels of petroleum, tons of coal, and megawatts of electricity and produce a meaningful sum. We must convert to a common unit of measure, most commonly the British Thermal Unit, or

BTU. A BTU is the amount of energy required to raise one pound of water one Fahrenheit degree under standard conditions. Thus the use of BTUs as an energy equivalent standard often is referred to as the heating value equivalent of a particular fuel, or the calorific equivalent.

It is common to see energy values represented as barrels (or tonnes) of oil equivalent. In such conversions, measures of nonoil fuels such as natural gas or coal are first translated into BTU energy equivalents. Then they are converted to oil equivalents using the average energy content of a barrel or tonne of oil.

Here we will work the other way, measuring countries' energy consumption totals in BTUs and converting petroleum consumption totals to the same unit of measure. Orders of magnitude are large in these totals—quadrillions, in fact. The shorthand unit of measure is "quads." One quad equals one quadrillion BTUs. This saves space. Here's how we'd have to write one quadrillion numerically: 1,000,000,000,000,000.

So how many BTUs does a barrel of crude oil contain? It varies among crude types. A standard average is 5.8 million BTUs per barrel of crude.

MEASURING ENERGY INTENSITIES

ow we know how to measure economic growth and energy consumption. To assess our three countries' energy efficiencies, then, we simply need to combine total energy consumption in a given year by economic output during that year. The result is what economists call "energy intensity."

Table 2–2 demonstrates the calculations for total energy and petroleum intensities for the United States, Japan, and Thailand during 1980–89.[4] The comparison involves two very industrialized countries and one that is rapidly industrializing.

Japan indeed uses energy more efficiently than the United States, partly for the reasons outlined earlier. Thailand seems to use energy more efficiently, but not petroleum. Does that mean that the United States wastes energy and petroleum, that Thailand wastes petroleum but not energy, and that Japan wastes nothing? Certainly not. Again, each country must be assessed in the context of its own circumstances.

The question should not be who wastes what, anyway. Analysis should address patterns of efficiency.

In the simplistic view of conservation, the United States seems not to have accomplished much in a comparison of the 1980 and 1989 energy and petroleum consumption totals. Energy consumption increased; petroleum consumption stayed about the same. Between those two years, however, GNP grew by 69%. Thus the energy intensity of the economy—the amount of energy required to produce a unit of economic growth—fell by 44%. And petroleum energy intensity declined by 47%.

This is very real conservation, even though consumption in absolute terms did not decline.

Japan performed better than that. Its energy intensity improved by 58% between 1980 and 1989, and its petroleum intensity improved by 64%. Thailand did not do as well. Its energy intensity improved by only 25%, its petroleum intensity by 33%.

TABLE 2-2
A BETTER WAY TO LOOK AT CONSERVATION:
ENERGY INTENSITY

Year	Primary energy consumption (Quads)	Petroleum consumption (Quads)	GNP (Million U.S. $)	Energy/ GNP (BTU/$)	Petroleum/ GNP (BTU/$)
U.S.					
1980	75.88	34.20	2,732,000	27,774	12,518
1981	73.88	31.93	3,052,700	24,202	10,460
1982	70.76	30.23	3,165,900	22,350	9,549
1983	70.41	30.05	3,405,700	20,674	8,823
1984	73.94	31.05	3,772,200	19,601	8,231
1985	73.75	30.92	4,014,900	18,369	7,701
1986	74.02	32.20	4,231,700	17,492	7,609
1987	76.59	32.87	4,524,200	16,929	7,265
1988	79.98	34.23	4,880,600	16,387	7,013
1989	81.14	34.21	*5,176,400	15,675	6,609
JAPAN					
1980	15.63	10.36	1,058,913	14,760	9,784
1981	15.43	10.04	1,164,492	13,250	8,662
1982	14.64	9.38	1,082,903	13,519	8,662
1983	14.50	8.97	1,181,239	12,275	7,594
1984	15.56	9.34	1,256,538	12,383	7,433
1985	15.75	8.90	1,330,762	11,835	6,688
1986	15.90	9.00	1,965,666	8,089	4,579
1987	16.42	9.08	2,387,251	6,878	3,804
1988	17.04	9.69	2,860,773	5,956	3,387
1989	17.54	10.11	*2,836,634	6,183	3,564
THAILAND					
1980	.51	.48	31,890	15,992	15,052
1981	.50	.45	34,290	14,581	13,123
1982	.48	.42	35,091	13,679	11,969
1983	.50	.44	39,278	12,730	11,202
1984	.56	.49	40,694	13,761	12,041
1985	.56	.47	36,701	15,258	12,806
1986	.60	.48	40,768	14,717	11,774
1987	.66	.53	47,100	14,013	11,253
1988	.69	.58	58,608	11,773	9,896
1989	.82	.69	*68,770	11,924	10,033

*Estimated
Source: Consumption and GNP data from *International Energy Statistics Sourcebook*, 1991, PennWell.

All three countries made conservation gains during the 1980s, different though the gains be. So how were the gains achieved?

Mainly, the decade opened with energy prices, especially petroleum, at historically high levels. As this chapter has shown, oil consumers respond to price rises by reducing their consumption. They did so with a vengeance in the 1980s.

Yet oil prices sagged in the early part of the 1980s, then crashed in 1986. And oil use efficiency continued to improve. Why?

The answer is simple. The high oil costs of the late 1970s and early 1980s made energy conservation investments attractive. Motorists made gasoline mileage considerations important factors in their vehicle purchase decisions. Businesses sought and found increasingly efficient ways to cool and heat working areas, to produce heat for chemical and manufacturing processes, to transport raw materials and products. These investments and many more like them changed the energy consumption infrastructure. The average annual pump price of unleaded gasoline in the United States was 12.4¢/gal less in 1989 than it was in 1980, in nominal terms. Motorists, however, did not trade in their compacts for gas guzzlers as a consequence. Moreover, what constituted a gas guzzler in 1989 was a far more efficient vehicle than its 1980 ancestor.

Due to past price jumps, therefore, the capital stock of the industrialized world is more efficient than it used to be and will remain that way no matter what prices do. Furthermore, people's habits have changed. Although consumers base their purchase decisions on price, their abilities to pay, and the intensities of their need, many intentionally conserve, at least in the sense of avoiding waste. The efficiency gains of the 1980s are permanent.

At this writing, one further consumption factor was at work around the world. Concern had become acute over the environmental effects of fossil fuel consumption. The concerns went beyond urban smog to alarm about possible atmospheric warming worldwide. Science raised considerable doubts about whether global warming really existed and whether fossil fuel combustion had anything to do with it. Nevertheless, the greenhouse gases that trap heat in the atmosphere, especially the carbon dioxide produced by fossil fuels combustion, have indeed increased in concentration. As a result, political pressures had grown for heavy taxes on the carbon contents of fossil fuels.

The likely outcome is uncertain. But international sentiment was high early in the 1990s for some significant reduction in consumption of fossil fuels, especially petroleum and coal. The purpose here is not to argue the merits of such a mandatory reduction but to point out what should by now be obvious: Such a reduction cannot come about except at the cost of economic growth. To be sure, where petroleum and coal are not burned, some other fuel will be. But petroleum and coal are burned now because they have economic advantages over other fuels. Mandatory substitution therefore involves costs, and those costs have economic effects that ought not be ignored.

In the 1980s, the economic mechanism of price produced impressive improvements in energy consumption efficiency. In the 1990s and beyond, environmental politics will play an increasing role in consumption patterns.

REFERENCES

1. *BP Statistical Review of World Energy*, British Petroleum Co. plc, 1992.

2. *Houston Chronicle*, August 30, 1992, p. 1E.

3. *Oil Market Report*, International Energy Agency, July 7, 1992.

4. Data from *International Energy Statistics Sourcebook*, PennWell Books, 1991.

CHAPTER THREE

SUPPLY:
THE
PROFESSIONAL
DIMENSION

Nearly every person in the world is an oil consumer. Yet relatively few of the world's inhabitants have much directly to do with oil supply. It is fairly easy to understand consumer behavior because most of us are consumers. It is, therefore, fairly easy to understand how consumer behavior comes to determine the aggregate market dimension known as demand.

Not so with supply. Supply is the professional dimension of the market. In the absence of some understanding of that dimension, it becomes too easy to perceive supply simply as the condition of oil's being available or not. In fact, supply is as dynamic as demand. It, too, responds to changes in economic conditions and does so continually.

Oil comes from rocks thousands or tens of thousands of feet underground. Rigs like this one, shown at work in East Texas, drill the holes that tap the oil-bearing rocks.

Chapter 1 portrayed the oil market as a closed system—a series of linked functions with physical limits and the perpetual need to constrain a fluid substance. In rough terms, supply is the system's size, the volume of oil inside it at a given time, and the speed at which the oil travels through it.

Oil Industry Structure

n understanding of supply requires some knowledge of the business that makes oil available in useful form to consumers. That business really is a collection of industries, each characterized by a unique profession.

What consumers know as gasoline, heating oil, lubricating oil, diesel, and other petroleum products start out as crude oil. In its natural state, crude oil has little value. For one thing, in its natural state, it usually is underground, where it can do no one any good. For another, its underground location begins as an unknown. Oil underground has no value, therefore, until someone first finds it and then conveys it to the Earth's surface, or at least proves that the conveyance is economically and technically feasible.

Even then, however, the crude has value only in its potential to be converted into useful fuels. Usually, crude as it comes out of the ground is dark, gooey stuff, mixed with mud and salt water and containing metals and perhaps sulfur and other chemicals. It might be black, green, brown, sometimes orange, or occasionally nearly clear. The really good stuff is nearly clear and very fluid, free of sulfur and other contaminants, approaching gasoline in chemical composition. The really bad stuff is so thick that it must be heated in order to flow, high in sulfur and metal content. To be worth anything, crude of any quality must be chemically transformed. The deliberate chemical change falls under a broad industry category called processing.

Crude oil, then, must be found, extracted, and processed. And between these steps it must be transported from place to place. The oil industry segment that searches for oil is called exploration. Extraction is called production. Processing is called refining. And transporting is called, well, transportation. These functions often are categorized as "upstream" or "downstream." The upstream business, including exploration and production, provides the oil industry's raw material. The downstream business is the manufacturing part of the industry; it takes the raw material, crude oil, and turns it into valuable products through the process of refining.

Professional disciplines differ widely among these various functions, which is why the industry seems so much like a collection of businesses to people familiar with it. Exploration, for example, employs the sciences of geophysics and geology. Production involves sophisticated engineering oriented to the behavior of oil-bearing layers of underground rock. In both upstream businesses, the crucial field activity is drilling, which is a professional and engineering specialty all its own.

Until the mid-1980s, the upstream industry segments tended to function discretely. A geophysicist produced a seismic section and interpreted it to produce a map of the underground. A geologist combined the geophysical information with field observations and information from any wells drilled in the study area to generate a "prospect"—a location to be drilled. Then a drilling crew, nowadays employees of a contractor and not the prospect-generating company, moved onto the location to drill a hole several thousand feet, or several tens of thousands of feet, into the ground to test the geologic theory. If the hole, or well, found oil in sufficient quantity, the production engineers took over to decide how best to get it out. The engineers' work led to field development, which normally included the drilling of more wells, installation of equipment to handle produced fluids, and perhaps a program of water injection or other method of enhancing production.

All these physical steps still must be performed. Since the mid-1980s, however, extremely powerful computers have made it possible for oil companies to blend information from each of the professional disciplines. Now, geophysicists work more closely with geologists than before in prospect generation, and petroleum engineers may enter the picture so that a prospective development program becomes available before the first well has been started, or "spudded," as they say in the field. The effect has been a blending of once-distinct functions, although the sequence of upstream steps has not changed much.

The downstream petroleum industry employs a different set of professionals, mainly chemists and engineers. Refining is a complex function that takes the generally big molecules that constitute crude oil and turns them into little, more useful molecules that can be mixed to make gasoline and other products. In general, chemists figure out what needs to be done, and refining engineers figure out how to do it. Related to their activities are those of marketing specialists who contrive ways to make consumers buy their

When oil companies make discoveries offshore they must install platforms to handle oil and gas production. This is a Shell-Esso platform in Eider field in the British North Sea. Photo courtesy of Royal Dutch/Shell Group.

products rather than those of competitors.

Connecting oil fields with refineries and refineries with service stations and home heating oil distributors is the transportation network. It includes tank trucks, ocean-going tankers, barges, pipelines, and storage facilities. Transportation, too, makes up a business unto itself. In fact, trucking, pipelining, and shipping are all very distinct businesses, each with its own professional specialty.

This, in very simple terms, is the mechanical part of the oil market, the industry that brings forth what economists call supply. We will examine the parts in greater detail later. What is important at this point is to recognize the unique characteristics of the petroleum supply functions and the people who perform them. Indeed, as hydrocarbon molecules pass from function to function, their ownership often changes. The number of ownership changes varies widely.

These disparities of function and ownership have important economic implications. They relate to the organization of companies, patterns of trade, and market behavior.

Some companies, for example, organize around particular functions. Thus there are independent producers, which specialize in upstream work. Their concentrations may be even more narrow; some independents focus on exploration, while some prefer to conduct only development and production operations. And there are independent refiners, which concentrate on processing and marketing.

Other companies organize around the concept of integration—ownership of both upstream and downstream operations. An integrated company thus finds and produces crude oil, refines it, and markets the products.

Integration introduces an interesting paradox of interests, the appreciation of which is crucial to an understanding of petroleum economics. High crude-oil prices benefit producers for obvious reasons: The producer of 20 B/D of crude makes more money when crude sells for $22/bbl than when the price falls to $15. To refiners, the crude-oil price is a feedstock cost. All else being equal—especially product prices—a refiner makes more money from $15/bbl crude than from its dearer alternative.

An integrated company looks at crude prices from both perspectives. At least in theory, it both sells crude (from its upstream divisions) and buys it (in its downstream units), even when the transactions occur internally. The advantages of integration have been the subjects of lively economic debate since John D. Rockefeller controlled the market. So, at times, has its legality. Whatever its other merits and drawbacks, integration brings into focus the vital dual nature of crude oil prices as both key determinant of producer revenues and principal cost for refiners.

THE DISTRIBUTION SYSTEM

C hapter 1 described the general flow of liquid hydrocarbons from the wellhead to the consumer. This chapter has described the general industry functions through which the hydrocarbons must pass and has pointed out that patterns of ownership change along the course. It is time now to put the general route and the functions together in an examination of the physical distribution system. The United States will serve as the example, since it is the world's single biggest petroleum market and since other distribution systems follow the general pattern.[1]

The U.S. distribution system has three parts. What is called the primary distribution system handles crude oil and products from the wellhead to large bulk terminals for petroleum products. The secondary distribution system divides the large quantities of product from large bulk terminals into smaller quantities for delivery to retail outlets and smaller bulk storage facilities. The tertiary system includes storage facilities and inventories of product consumers (Fig. 3–1).

The primary distribution system begins at the lease tank, a storage unit near the producing well. Crude oil moves from there into gathering pipelines or tank trucks. Gathering pipelines may connect to larger trunk pipelines or to loading stations for trucks, barges, or rail tank cars. The crude may travel to a storage terminal or directly to a refinery, where it usually spends more time in a storage tank. Imported crude oil arrives by tanker for unloading at marine terminals, which have storage capacity and pipeline links to refineries or trunk pipelines. Crude oil purchased by the U.S. government goes into salt dome storage facilities of the Strategic Petroleum Reserve.

Refineries have storage tanks for crude, intermediate products (those requiring further processing), and finished products. The finished products move from refinery storage by pipeline, tank truck, barge, or tanker toward a general market area, stopping usually at the large bulk terminal that represents the end of the primary distribution system.

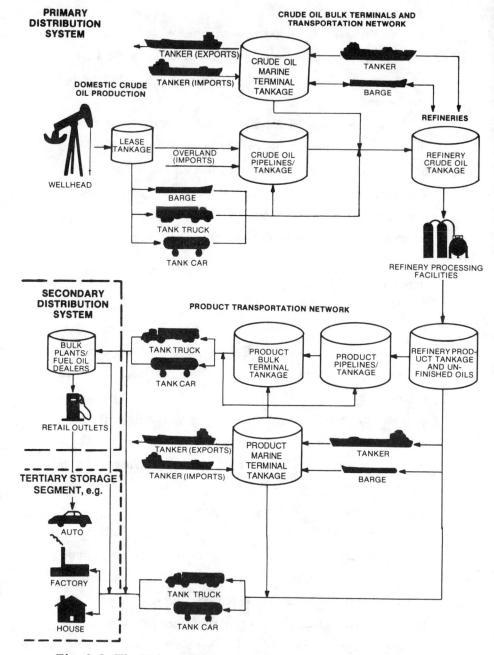

Fig. 3–1. The U.S. petroleum distribution system (courtesy of National Petroleum Council).

The secondary distribution system includes localized storage facilities and retail outlets. The storage at this stage usually involves wholesale bulk plants that receive products by tank car or truck. From wholesale storage, products move to tanks at retail outlets, including service stations and retail fuel oil dealers.

Storage in the tertiary distribution system includes everything from fuel tanks for boilers at factories to fuel oil tanks in homes, to gasoline tanks in automobiles. Sometimes, products move directly from the primary distribution system to the tertiary system. High-volume fuel users often invest in direct transportation links to the primary system in order to avoid the costs of the secondary system. Large airlines, for example, purchase jet fuel directly from refineries where logistics are favorable.

Downstream of refineries, product ownership can change several times. Especially in the case of gasoline, this is not always apparent because of widespread brand identification with oil companies. A motorist filling up at a service station identified by the brand of a major refiner indeed buys that refiner's gasoline, but the station attendant may or may not be an employee of the refiner. In fact, the attendant probably works for an independent business person who owns the station and pays for the right to use the refiner's brand. The station owner might also be a management company operating stations on behalf of the refiner.

In 1985, 81.5% of gasoline sales by all refiners were to independent dealers or wholesalers, called jobbers. Service stations operated by refining company employees accounted for only 16.4% of total gasoline sales. The rest of the sales were to bulk purchasers.[2]

When crude oil comes out of the ground, then, it and its

derivatives most likely will have several owners before a consumer buys the finished products. Each of these changes in ownership implies a business transaction. Petroleum rings many cash registers as it passes through its essential production, processing, and distribution system.

THE
NOTION
OF
CAPACITY

Because it is a closed system, the market at any given time can handle only so much oil. The limit is its capacity. And the market's ultimate capacity to deliver petroleum products to consumers represents the sum of the physical capacities of the industry's various functions.

Thus there are production capacity, pipeline capacity, refining capacity, and storage capacity. In theory, there must be some limit to how much gasoline retail outlets can dispense in a given time, although the market seldom approaches it except in isolated cases where significant numbers of outlets cease to function for some reason.

Nature and money determine capacities. Nature determined the extent and location of Earth's endowment of crude oil. Money determines the vigor of the effort to find crude and the extent of investment in production, transportation, refining, and storage equipment. Furthermore, the availability of money for operations performed by that equipment depends greatly on prices of crude and petroleum products, which in turn depend greatly, though not entirely, on demand. Consumer power looms again.

Production capacity is a function of reserves and the capital invested in producing equipment. The term "reserves" is important. It means the amount of oil known with fair certainty to exist underground that can be produced under current economic conditions with current technology. "Reserves" usually means "proved reserves," although there is no such thing as "unproved" reserves, except, perhaps, in hybrid reporting schemes. There are, however, such queer birds as "probable" and "possible" reserves. These perplexities of reserves will be discussed in more detail in Chapter 5. What's important here is to understand that reserves estimates have to do with crude known to lie underground but involve quantities that vary as crude oil prices change, as investments are made in producing equipment, and as more becomes known about the oil-bearing rock, or reservoir.

The rate at which oil can be produced from a given field depends upon a number of factors. Some have to do with the nature of the reservoir rock: how much pressure exists within it, how readily oil can pass through it, how fluid the oil is, and so forth. It is possible to ruin oil fields by producing crude oil too fast, a practice that prematurely exhausts natural pressures and renders much of the oil in place unproducible. Petroleum engineers determine optimum rates and methods of production.

Within those natural constraints, economics determines the rate and extent of field development, which involves the drilling of production wells and installation of production equipment. A company seldom makes all its investment in a field at once. Usually, it drills enough wells and installs enough equipment to bring the field on stream at some rate that generates an acceptable level of cash flow. Then, as initial investments are recovered, subsequent phases of development may be undertaken to increase or maintain production. The decision parameters are complicated. Crude prices, and expectations for them, are crucial.

Once a field is on stream, its production capacity at any given time is the maximum rate, usually in barrels per day, at which it can produce on a sustained basis, given the reservoir's characteristics and the equipment installed to handle production. A company increases capacity by spending money to find and develop reserves and to increase the maximum producing rate of existing reserves. If those investments are not made, capacity shrinks because reserves deplete, underground pressures subside, natural flowing rates decline, and equipment turns old and rusty.

Often, production capacities are reported in two subcategories. One is a maximum, flat-out rate called a surge capacity. Fields cannot produce at surge capacity for extended periods for a number of reasons. Among those reasons are pressure problems with producing reservoirs and the inability of equipment to operate at maximum rates forever. The more meaningful production capacity figure is the maximum sustainable producing rate. As the name implies, it measures the highest rate of production that can be maintained without damaging the underground reservoir and with proper allowance for equipment maintenance, replacement, and operating necessities.

The capacities of transportation and storage functions are easier to visualize than those of production. Pipelines have maximum volumes. Petroleum can pass through them at rates that depend mostly on pipe diameters, the power of pumping equipment installed, the resistance to flow (or viscosity) of the petroleum itself, and the extent of efforts to reduce friction between the fluid and pipeline walls. Tanks have obvious volume limits. Capacities in each case depend on investments. When more storage is necessary, tank owners build more tanks. When more transportation is necessary, pipeline owners install more pumps, up to certain limits, or lay new pipelines. Sometimes, the new pipelines are laid alongside existing lines in a process called looping.

Refining capacities are more complicated. A modern refinery involves a number of processes, each designed to either break down or rearrange hydrocarbon molecules. The basic process, the first main step in refining, is distillation. In it, crude oil—and to a much lesser extent other inputs such as natural gas condensates—is heated to the point of boiling at the bottom of a tall tower. Vapors rise through the tower, cooling along the way. Heavier, less volatile substances condense first and are collected in trays and carried out of the tower. Lighter components of crude, or fractions, condense later—higher in the tower. Some fractions never condense and leave the tower as gases.

Basic refining capacity thus measures the maximum amount of crude a plant's distillation towers can handle in a given period. Crude capacity must be distinguished from total refinery capacity, which includes noncrude feedstocks. Capacities are measured in barrels per stream day, which is the maximum processing rate during a period of operation, or barrels per calendar day, which are generally based on a year's operating averages and include normal downtime for maintenance and repairs.

Obviously, a refiner can add capacity by building more distillation capacity. To the extent distillation capacity is limited by some physical constriction of a product stream, the refiner also can add capacity by widening or eliminating the constriction. This process is called debottlenecking.

Capacities of refining processes downstream of distillation are increasingly important to petroleum economics. The market increasingly wants more light products, such as gasoline and jet fuel, than result from the distillation process, and less of the heavy ones, such as residual oil, which doesn't evaporate during distillation (see Table 3–1). Refineries therefore have processes for turning the lower-value products of distillation into higher-value products. They are called upgrading capacities and include such technological marvels as catalytic cracking, hydrocracking, and delayed coking. A rough way to gauge the relative refining sophistication of plants, countries, or regions is to compare their ratios of distillation capacity to upgrading capacity. Allowances must be made, however, for disparities of demand and feedstock. Less upgrading capacity is needed in regions of comparatively less gasoline demand, for example. Similarly, a refinery with ready access to high quality crude does not require as much upgrading capacity as a less fortunate counterpart serving the same products market.

Deciding what types of processes to install in a refinery, or how to modify existing processes, is complex. Planners have to predict demand patterns for the various petroleum products and decide how to match refining processes to their market projections. The ability to invest at all depends on current and expected refining profitability, which is a function of crude costs, product prices, and operating expenses.

TABLE 3-1
THE LIGHTENING OF OIL PRODUCTS USED IN THE U.S.

Year	Finished motor gasoline	Naphtha jet fuel	Kerosine jet fuel	Kerosine	Distillate fuel oil	Residual fuel oil	Other products
			Share of U.S. product consumption—percent				
1970	39.4	1.7	4.9	1.8	17.3	15.0	19.9
1971	39.5	1.7	4.9	1.6	17.5	15.1	19.6
1972	39.0	1.5	4.9	1.4	17.8	15.5	20.0
1973	38.6	1.3	4.9	1.2	17.9	16.3	20.0
1974	39.3	1.3	4.6	1.1	17.7	15.8	20.2
1975	40.9	1.1	4.8	1.0	17.5	15.1	19.5
1976	40.0	1.1	4.5	1.0	17.9	16.0	19.4
1977	38.9	1.1	4.5	1.0	18.2	16.7	19.6
1978	39.3	1.1	4.6	0.9	18.2	16.0	19.9
1979	38.0	1.3	4.7	1.0	17.9	15.3	22.0
1980	38.6	1.2	5.0	0.9	16.8	14.9	22.7
1981	41.0	1.4	5.0	0.8	17.6	13.0	21.3
1982	42.8	1.4	5.3	0.8	17.5	11.2	21.1
1983	43.5	1.4	5.5	0.8	17.7	9.3	21.8
1984	42.6	1.4	6.1	0.7	18.1	8.7	22.4
1985	43.4	1.4	6.4	0.7	18.2	7.6	22.2
1986	43.2	1.2	6.8	0.6	17.9	8.7	21.5
1987	43.2	1.2	7.1	0.6	17.9	7.6	22.4
1988	42.4	1.2	7.2	0.6	18.1	8.0	22.6
1989	42.3	1.2	7.4	0.5	18.2	7.9	22.5

Source: Author's calculations from U.S. Bureau of Mines, Energy Information Administration data published in *Energy Statistics Sourcebook,* PennWell, 1990.

THE
SUPPLY
QUESTION

C hapter 1 proposed three questions central to any assessment of petroleum market behavior. The first involved the world's need for oil products and related to demand. The second involved the world's ability and willingness to deliver oil to market. That's the question of supply, some of the dimensions of which this chapter has tried to describe.

In assessing supply, it is important to remember that the petroleum market is a closed system. As a worldwide group, producers, refiners, and transporters seldom can deliver supply at will. Just as nature despises a vacuum, the market despises shortage; in fact, it will not allow shortage to develop. To that end, it tries constantly to ensure that the sum of physical production, refining, and transportation capacities—the world's ability to deliver oil to market—exceeds demand. And it usually succeeds. Almost always, the world can deliver more oil to market than the market wants. Another way of saying this is that demand usually constrains supply. That is our working definition of "surplus." Indeed, surplus is the market's normal state.

The supply dimension of the market thus seldom operates at capacity. The market demands that there be surplus capacity at every operational stage of the system to accommodate unexpected surges in demand. It pays for that capacity. When supply approaches capacity, the condition of surplus begins to give way to shortage—that unusual circumstance in which supply works to constrain demand. What happens then? Prices rise.

If the approaching condition of shortage relates to crude oil, crude prices rise. When that happens, production investments become more profitable, and capital flows to them. Explorers drill more wells and find more reserves. Producers install more gas/oil separation equipment and pumping units. Production capacity increases. Sooner or later, supply no longer threatens to function as a limit to demand; the shortage gives way to the blessed normalcy of surplus.

The same thing happens when the shortage relates to the deliverability of products by refiners. When demand approaches refining capacity and inventories diminish, shortage threatens, product prices rise, and new distillation units or debottlenecking projects begin to look like good investments.

The reverse occurs, as well. When demand falls in relation to supply, some measure of capacity must be idled lest storage tanks fill to the point of overflowing. Wells must be shut in. Refineries must operate at diminishing percentages of their maximum rates. When the condition lasts a long time, operators plug wells, which usually means they never can flow again. Refineries close. Indeed, refinery closings removed 16% of U.S. refining capacity during the product demand slump of the 1980s (see Table 3–2). Chapter 4 will examine the interactions of price, supply, and demand in more detail and show how they affect decisions regarding capacity.

Swings in capacity totals and utilization rates are important ways the market adjusts to changing circumstances of supply and demand, shortage and surplus. When it asks how much oil the world can or will deliver and the answer seems too close to that of

TABLE 3–2
HOW U.S. REFINING CAPACITY
SHRINKS WITH DEMAND

Year	Total products demand	Operable refining capacity*
	(Thousands of barrels per day)	
1970	14,697.2	12,860.2
1971	15,212.5	13,292.5
1972	16,367.0	13,671.4
1973	17,307.7	14,361.5
1974	16,652.7	14,960.7
1975	16,322.0	15,236.6
1976	17,461.1	16,398.4
1977	18,431.4	17,047.7
1978	18,846.6	17,440.9
1979	18,516.0	17,991.1
1980	17,055.9	18,620.5
1981	16,057.7	17,889.7
1982	15,295.7	16,859.3
1983	15,231.1	16,137.1
1984	15,725.6	15,658.8
1985	15,726.4	15,459.0
1986	16,280.6	15,565.5
1987	16,665.0	15,915.4
1988	17,283.3	15,654.9
1989	17,325.2	15,572.0

*As of December 31 of each year.
Source: *Energy Statistics Sourcebook.*

the demand question, prices rise, unused capacities are pressed into operation, and capital flows to investments needed to make capacities themselves increase. The role of money is crucial here. But where is it not?

REFERENCES

1. *Petroleum Storage and Transportation,* Vol. 1, National Petroleum Council, 1989.

2. *Gasoline Marketing and Divorcement: A Background Primer,* American Petroleum Institute, October 1987.

CHAPTER FOUR

WHO SETS THE PRICE?

Market forces—supply, demand, and price—never hold still. They constantly affect and are affected by one another. Furthermore, they never are free from outside influence. Supply, demand, and price never change for the sake of change. They change for some reason: a war that halts crude oil production in a major exporting country, an unusually cold winter in several major consuming regions, imposition of oil consumption taxes, fluctuations in economic activity.

An appreciation for the connections between these influences is crucial to accurate assessments of market change. The first three chapters demonstrated how the forces act on one another but

The oil market's two principal segments—crude oil and products—come together at the refinery. This is where chemistry turns a raw natural substance into gasoline, heating oil, and other fuels. Shown here is the BHP Petroleum Americas refinery on Oahu, Hawaii. Note the storage tanks, where crude awaits distillation, where intermediate products await further processing, and where finished products await transport to market. Photo courtesy of BHP Petroleum Americas.

treated them individually in terms of benchmark questions: How much oil does the world need? How much oil can or will the world deliver to market? Important as it is to answer those questions in assessing the market, stopping with isolated answers is never enough.

The temptation is always strong to paralyze one of the forces, assert change in another, and solve for price. Demand goes up, so price must go up. Supply goes up, so price must go down.

Well, maybe. But the market does not work that way. Supply and demand fluctuate. Prices need not rise because demand jumps. What if supply jumps, too? And if supply goes up, prices might not move at all if demand rises in step. A perceptive analyst learns to assess the market's elemental forces in relation to one another, to look beyond the news event that created the latest change in supply or demand.

Let's assume war breaks out (again) in the Middle East, shutting in, say, 2 million B/D of crude oil production. In a 60 million B/D worldwide market, that is enough to raise alarm. What happens to price?

It jumps—for a while, anyway. The price increase might not last even a day. Or it might last for weeks or several months. Why the difference?

It depends on conditions of supply and demand prior to the supply interruption. If crude and product storage tanks were full (in economic parlance, if stocks were high), withdrawals from inventory would offset much of the production loss for perhaps a couple of months. That buys time for idle production capacity outside the troubled area to swing on stream—assuming any such idle capacity exists. If, on the other hand, stocks were low and production was at capacity when the war began, a 2 million B/D supply interruption would mean volumes truly lost and not quickly replaced.

Just as important to the market's response is demand behavior preceding the jolt. If the worldwide economy was going gangbusters prior to the war, demand probably was rising. A lost 2 million B/D would mean something quite different in those circumstances than it would mean in conditions of economic torpor, with demand sagging and consumers' abilities to afford oil diminishing.

What is more, if prices do rise appreciably, and if they do remain at their elevated levels for long, the market makes further adjustments. Some number of consumers resided at the economic margin before the market upset: They were paying all they could afford for oil at the former price. Now that prices have jumped, they must quit consuming or consume at lower rates. Demand begins to decline. That, too, will affect price at some point, depending on what happens to supply.

And so on. The market never rests.

WHY DO PRICES JUMP?

egardless of market conditions, however, prices seem always to jump whenever there's a supply interruption—or even the rumor of one. And newspapers send their junior reporters out to ask service station owners why oil companies are gouging consumers again. Suspicion deepens later when no one seems to have been able to find empty pipelines or other unassailable evidence of shortage.

It is true that prices spurt when supply sources come under threat, especially when demand was on the rise beforehand. And there is a very good reason why they do.

Chapter 3 pointed out an important bias of the market: It detests shortage. More than that, it loves surplus. The market is calm when demand constrains supply; it goes berserk when the reverse becomes the case. Indeed, the market simply will not tolerate shortage by our definition of the term. Economists speak of equilibrium, that hypothetical balance of supply, demand, and price that the market constantly pursues yet never manages to catch and hold. The oil market would not abide such a balance; it would demand that there be some oil in inventory, some idle production capacity at the ready, some unused refining and transportation capacity.

The closed system needs breathing room.

This bias toward surplus results from the many articulations of function and ownership that lie between crude oil in the reservoir and product in the carburetor or heating element. Nearly every step represents a potential business transaction, a sale by the producer to the pipeline owner, by the pipeline owner to the refiner, by the refiner to the bulk terminal operator, and so on. It does not happen that way with every barrel of crude oil, of course. An integrated company might own some quantity of petroleum from the wellhead to the gasoline pump—but not much. Most petroleum changes hands once, twice, or more likely several times as it passes through the system.

And what is on the minds of owners at each step? Today's price and tomorrow's supply. Petroleum producers, transporters, and processors, whether they're independent or integrated, want always to make current sales volumes produce as much revenue as possible. That is simple business. But they want just as intently to know they will have oil to sell in the future and someone willing to buy it. They must constantly attend to replacement supply.

Concern for replacement supply is a primal motivation in the oil business. It is the reason oil-producing companies undertake the tremendous risks and inconveniences of exploration. It is the reason for tanks at refineries, bulk terminals, and retail outlets. The people who buy and sell petroleum, wherever they reside in the market, cannot afford ever to be caught with nothing to offer customers. Sellers quickly run out of customers when they run out of the goods that they sell. Hence the bulges in the system: the tanks and other storage facilities as well as, in normal circumstances, a safety cushion of spare capacity at nearly every stage.

Buyers and sellers need to know that if demand takes a surprise turn upward, or if supply slumps unexpectedly from normal sources, a pull on inventories or mobilization of spare capacity can take up the slack. At the first sign that conditions are straining available capacity somewhere in the system—that production is approaching maximum rates or that refineries are operating at nearly total capacity utilization rates—buyers and sellers worry about replacement supply. In order to maintain deliveries to their customers, they intensify competition for what is available. They bid higher prices for what they buy for processing or resale. Ultimately, they must pass the higher prices on to their customers or sacrifice profits. Usually, they do a little of both.

In an age of computer communications and instant news, an event triggering fears for replacement supply can have dramatic effects. For each buyer and seller in the market, after all, failure to replace goods sold can mean the difference between commercial survival and, as the euphemism goes, the opportunity to pursue new interests. Upsets large enough to generate widespread fears do not happen every day, or even every month. When they do occur, however, prices can leap with lightning speed, remaining elevated at least until the market has the chance to assess the extent of the threat to replacement supply.

The charge is often made that prices seldom fall back to pre-crisis levels as rapidly as they rose when the upset happened. This may be true, although some studies claim it is not. If it is, the explanation is simple: The commercial penalty a petroleum seller faces for coming up short is more severe than the extra cost of holding too much in inventory.

Moreover, price leaps—or spikes—must be viewed in historic perspective. It is concern for replacement supply at every point of potential commercial transaction that creates the market's intolerance for shortage and preference for surplus. To repeat, when the system approaches capacity, concerned buyers and sellers bid up prices to levels sufficient to encourage greater purchases for storage and creation of new capacity, be it production, processing, transportation, or all three. The market's normal condition is a demand constraint on supply, or surplus. Concern for replacement supply keeps it that way.

What happens to price in conditions of surplus? It remains at levels barely tolerable to producers (in the case of crude) or refiners, wholesalers, and retailers (in the case of products). Again, the reason is easy to understand. In normal conditions, somebody, if not everybody, has too much capacity. The market demands it. Idle capacity costs money; it represents invested capital not generating returns; it requires maintenance. Producers recognize the necessity for spare capacity, but they would prefer that their competitors maintain it. Refiners feel the same way.

So there are, let us say, 20 refiners with five units of idle capacity each in a market that has not changed much for months. Suddenly, demand increases by one unit. Twenty refiners each increase throughput by one unit, creating 19 units of product the market does not need. The refiners must choose whether to sell cheap or store unneeded product. Price slumps.

It is never that simple, of course. But a market with much spare capacity behaves this way, characteristically overreacting to signs of increasing demand and further weakening price. Too much spare capacity can make the market appear to work backward, with demand increases leading (at first) to lower prices—until the demand increase restores capacity utilization rates to healthy levels.

What have we said here? In the market's normal condition of surplus, there is a bias toward price weakness. In normal conditions, there is more room for prices to fall than to rise—until capacity surpluses shrink appreciably. The shrinkage can occur in two ways: durable demand growth or capacity eliminations by distressed owners. In periods when nothing seems to threaten replacement supply, meaning most of the time, these tensions moderate prices at every level.

When apprentice reporters interview service station owners during unusual market circumstances, however, this part of the story—the downside price bias that prevails when conditions are normal—seldom gets remembered.

TYPES OF OIL, TYPES OF PRICES

Although it is quite normal to hear mention of "the oil price," no such thing exists. There is no single price of oil.

The term "oil" can mean crude oil or petroleum products. Generally, products are worth more than crude for the same reason that bread is worth more than wheat. Processing adds value.

Even when the chemical distinctions are clear, prices for a single product vary from region to region. Gasoline prices, posted as they are in most places for all the world to see, can vary from one urban intersection to the next and usually do. The same holds true for heating oil, lubricants, and crude oil itself. Patterns of supply and demand vary geographically. Economic health changes from place to place.

Furthermore, crudes vary tremendously in quality and composition. Just as there are grades of gasoline—regular, midgrade, and premium—so are there grades of crude. But there are more of them for crude than there are for gasoline—many more. And the market must sort out the differences.

The main parameters of crude quality are density and sulfur content. Density is measured by something called API gravity, which is expressed in degrees. Crudes with relatively high API gravities are considered light; those with lower API gravities are heavy. There also are medium or intermediate weights.

Cutoffs between the "light," "medium," and "heavy" categories apply mainly to crudes within particular families, which have names. For example, Iraq exports three crudes in the Basrah family: Basrah Heavy with an API gravity of 24.7°; Basrah Medium, 31.1°; and Basrah Light, 33.7°. In general, heavy crudes have API gravities below 25°; mediums have API gravities of 25–32°; lights have API gravities higher than that.

Everything else being equal, light crudes are more valuable than medium or heavy crudes because they produce comparatively greater quantities of light, high-value products such as gasoline and light distillates, in distillation. The technical way of saying this is that they have lighter, higher-value distillation yields.

Sulfur content is measured as a simple weight percent. Crudes with more than 1.5% sulfur are considered sour. Those containing less sulfur are said to be sweet. Sweet crudes, because they don't require the added cost of desulfurization in processing, have higher values.

Grades of crude by these main determinants of value range from heavy and sour on the low end to light and sweet on the high. There are other factors of crude quality, such as volatility, pour point, viscosity, and concentrations of metals and other materials. In the market, however, density and sulfur content are by far the most common quality measures.

A common and important term heard in market circles is "netback value." This is a theoretical measure of the value of a particular crude to a particular refiner or group of refiners in a particular market, based on going product prices and net of operating and transit costs. Published netback values use refinery configurations typical to a region. Thus U.S. Gulf Coast netbacks, like those calculated for Northwest Europe, assume relatively high cracking capacities in relation to total distillation. In the Asia-Pacific refining center of Singapore, hydroskimming is more common than cracking, which means refineries there make proportionately less gasoline and more heavier products. Netback calculations use these assumptions to postulate an average composite product barrel, then price out that hypothetical barrel on the basis of current product prices. That's the netback.

Except for the most specialized ones, market information services do not attempt to report prices for every type of crude traded. Instead, they cover crudes considered representative of particular refining centers. At Rotterdam in the Netherlands, for example, Brent crude from the North Sea is a normal benchmark. Brent also is quoted on the U.S. Gulf Coast, along with West Texas Intermediate and Alaskan North Slope. In Singapore, Dubai Fateh crude serves as a marker crude. In general, other crudes trade against these and other markers, with adjustments for quality differences. Price variances of one crude against a marker are called differentials, which must be calculated for haul distances as well as quality.

Within the Organization of Petroleum Exporting Countries, Saudi Arabian Light crude once functioned as a benchmark. In recent years, the exporters' group has used a so-called basket of eight crudes in establishing its price targets.

Price quotations for marker crudes at specified refining centers are usually spot prices. That is, they are the prices refiners pay for marginal volumes of crude, generally purchased cargo by cargo. They are distinguished from term prices, which are determined by contracts for continuous deliveries. Refiners once relied on term purchases for most feedstock needs to assure continuity of supply and used spot purchases to fill temporary shortfalls. In recent years they have tended to rely on spot purchases for more of their basic feedstock needs than before so as not to get locked into long term commitments to buy crude at prices that may prove higher than the market. Since spot purchases by nature represent marginal supply they are considered most representative of the market in which they are made at the time of transaction.

Quotes for spot transactions at refining centers usually are *cif* prices. The acronym stands for "cargo, insurance, and freight." Cif prices thus represent not just the price of the crude but also the costs of transporting it to market. "Delivered" prices are similar but include additional costs, such as those of clearing customs.

At the other end of the scale are *fob* prices. Another acronym: "free on board." The oil market usually assumes this to mean fob seller. The fob price represents crude costs at a seller's loading terminal to a buyer paying his own transportation, insurance, and other expenses. It should be obvious that cif prices vary with distance to market. When the fob price for Saudi Light crude is $17/bbl, for example, its cif price on the U.S. Gulf Coast exceeds its cif price in Rotterdam because of the greater haul distance. Like crude prices, product prices are quoted on both fob and cif bases.

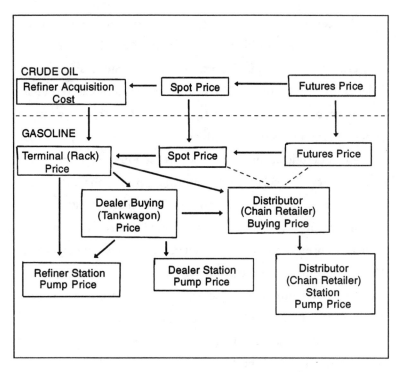

Fig. 4–2. Types of oil prices (courtesy of American Petroleum Institute).

Product markets have different types of price, too (Fig. 4–2). The different prices reflect the potential layers of ownership downstream of the refinery. In the United States, gasoline has a "rack price," which is a wholesale price at a terminal or refinery truck loading facility (called a "rack") to nonbranded, independent marketers. The rack price is considered gasoline's commodity price. Gasoline also has a "dealer tankwagon price," which a dealer pays to his supplier for bulk deliveries to his outlet. The supplier may be a refinery or wholesaler. And there's a "street price," or retail price, of gasoline, which includes taxes. This is also called the "pump price." In regional comparisons of retail gasoline prices, it is important to pay attention to taxes, which vary greatly.

Just as there are different types of petroleum products, there are different types of crude and different categories of price for both crude and products. To review, some crude changes hands under continuous contract. In recent years, cargo by cargo transactions have come to dominate the market. Quotes for contract crude are term prices; for cargo by cargo deals they are spot prices. The price of crude at the loading port is the fob price. A price that includes costs of carriage to the unloading port is the cif price. A price that represents the composite product barrel likely to result from the crude is the netback price; normally theoretical, netback pricing has been used as a way to guarantee profits for refiner-purchasers and thus to promote crude sales. And when OPEC ministers haggle over production quotas, the target price they discuss is really an average of the fob prices for eight OPEC crudes.

Obviously, it is important for market observers to understand these distinctions. And there are others.

Individual markets have developed characteristic mechanics. Where refineries are located close to production, refiners publish bids for the various types of crude accessible to them. These are called "posted prices."

In many regions, forward markets have developed, often as a way to accommodate physical loading limits. A well-known example is the informal but very active market for the Brent blend of crudes from a cluster of fields in the northern North Sea. This market covers crude carried ashore by pipeline to a terminal at Sullom Voe in the United Kingdom's Shetland Islands. Some Brent crude is traded on a normal spot basis; cargoes changing hands this way are referred to as dated. In a dated Brent deal, the transaction is made, and delivery occurs within a specific period. In forward

Brent trading, the delivery time is less certain. Transactions in this system are called 15-day Brent deals and involve agreements made in the first 15 days of one month for delivery in a following month. Thus delivery in a Brent deal occurs at least 16 days after the purchase. The 15-day scheme evolved as an accommodation to mechanical operation of the Sullom Voe terminal.

The Brent forward market involves trading in "wet" and "paper" barrels. Wet barrels are physical cargoes. Paper barrels are agreements to buy or deliver physical cargoes. Paper trading becomes possible when, as is the case in the Brent forward market, sufficient time—usually at least a month—transpires between the sales/purchase agreement and the delivery of crude.

Forward trading bridges another important distinction in this complicated world of oil prices: that between physical and futures trading. As the name suggests, physical trading involves real barrels and cargoes of oil, what the Brent market calls wet barrels. Futures trading involves contracts, not physical oil; hence it is often called the paper-barrel market. A futures contract is an agreement to deliver a specified quantity of crude oil (or gasoline or heating oil) at a specified place on a specified future date. The seller agrees to make the delivery; the buyer to take delivery. In reality, most futures traders usually don't contemplate physical movement of crude. On the International Petroleum Exchange in Europe, in fact, there is no provision for physical crude oil deliveries, which is not to say contract holders cannot physically consummate the agreements if they so choose. Usually, futures traders annul delivery obligations by buying or selling offsetting contracts. Thus the holder of a futures contract approaching expiration sells a contract with reciprocal commitments, and no physical delivery need occur.

Futures trading in crude oil and key products developed rapidly in the 1980s. Chapter 9 will discuss the subject in more detail. At this point it is important to recognize the extent to which futures trading opens a window on the oil market. Transactions occur on formal exchanges; the biggest are Europe's IPE and the New York Mercantile Exchange. So, unlike the diverse spot market, all the trading takes place in one place, which makes it possible to follow prices transaction by transaction. And the futures market, unencumbered as it is by the hardware necessities of physicals trading, reacts instantaneously to events with the potential for upsetting physical markets. Futures trading thus makes the market more "transparent" than it was when all trading involved wet barrels.

"So who sets the price of oil?" someone inevitably asks, wanting a comprehensible answer that can be condensed into a sentence or two. When the victim of such an inquiry is a person who understands all the forces at work in the oil market and all the things "price of oil" can mean, the best answer is an indulgent smile and polite change of subject.

WHERE
THE
MARKETS
MEET

ne more concept is crucial to an understanding of petroleum price movements. It has to do with the point where the commodity and product dimensions of the market converge.

Those dimensions are, in effect, separate but related markets. Someone buying gasoline or heating oil in Milwaukee really cares little about OPEC politics, reservoir performance on Alaska's North Slope, or anything else that might influence the market for crude. And, as the world has often seen, OPEC oil ministers at times display dangerously haphazard regard for motorists in Milwaukee.

Product consumers ultimately determine demand for crude oil, just as crude oil producers ultimately determine supply. As we have seen, however, the intermediate steps are crucial. And the crucial economic point in these intermediate steps is the refiner's margin.

This is the fundamental measure of refining profitability. The margin measures the differences between the refiner's revenues from sales of petroleum products and all his expenses, including the cost of crude. Operating expenses do not change as much as crude and product prices. So the size of the margin—indeed, whether one exists at all—depends mostly on constantly varying crude costs on the one hand and product prices on the other.

The basic margin calculation subtracts the average price a refiner is paying for crude from the average netback value. As discussed earlier, the netback is the revenue realization from the average composite product barrel, less operating and transportation costs. Refining margins can be negative. Refiners will sell product at a loss during highly competitive periods in order to maintain market share. But they cannot do so indefinitely.

Refining margins are extremely important indicators of market health. Narrow or nonexistent margins mean some sort of imbalance between crude and product values. When refiners are having difficulty selling product and must lower their sales prices, their margins obviously narrow. That in turn makes them seek lower prices for their crude purchases. Sometimes they can find cheaper crude, sometimes not. If there's a lot of excess crude capacity when product prices turn weak, chances are the beleaguered refiner will find someone willing to sell cheap in order to move crude. When producers are operating at near capacity, crude discounts turn scarce. Product market slumps under periods of crude market health mean refining losses.

Refining profitability is an important market indicator. Analysts estimate it in a variety of ways. One basic method calculates a netback value for crude based on prices of two major products under assumptions about yields of those products in a refinery typical of the region under consideration. In the United States, a modern refinery can turn 60% of the crude barrel into gasoline and most of the remaining 40% into distillate product. An estimate of U.S. refining profitability, therefore, might subtract the spot crude price from a 60/40 gasoline/fuel oil netback value based on spot prices for those products (Table 4–1). Typical per-barrel operating and transit costs can be subtracted from the resulting margin to produce a rough estimate of regional refining profitability. Outside the United States, different product yields are necessary because distillate in most countries accounts for more of the product barrel than does gasoline. The profitability calculation's validity depends on how closely the product split approximates regional average refining yields.

Futures market analysts use a similar gauge of refining profitability called the crack spread. It compares the value of a certain number of barrels of crude with the same number of barrels of two or more products, the product barrel total being split to approximate regional refining yields. In the United States, the most common such calculation is the 3-2-1 crack spread, which measures the

---

TABLE 4–1
ONE WAY TO ESTIMATE REFINING PROFITABILITY

Spot prices, New York Harbor:

Brent crude	$19.50/bbl
Motor gasoline	$27/bbl
No. 2 Heating oil	$25/bbl

Value of the product barrel assuming 60% gasoline yield, 40% heating oil yield:

$27 x .6 =	$16.20
$25 x .4 =	+ 10.00
	$26.20

Less:

Transit	- $0.80	
Process	- 2.50	
		- 3.30
Netback value		$22.90
Less crude cost		- 19.50
Hypothetical margin		3.40

---

difference (or spread) between the value of 3 bbl of crude and the value of 2 bbl of gasoline plus 1 bbl of distillate fuel oil. Values can be based on spot or futures prices.

As long as crude and product prices and refining yields are representative of the refining center for which the analysis is performed, margin estimates based on crack spread calculations like these usually represent a valid market gauge. They never reflect profits for a particular refinery, of course, since plant yields and crude use patterns vary. But crude/product spread calculations do show whether market conditions at least make it possible for refiners to earn profits.

Refiners, like producers, have to manage capacity utilization in accordance with their concerns for profitability and market share. When product markets are weak, refiners reduce runs, using less of their capacity. Doing so effectively reduces supply and eventually should strengthen product prices and refining margins. For competitive reasons, however, one refiner might keep producing at money-losing rates for a while, hoping the refiner across town will reduce runs and create a chance to lure customers away with lower prices. That is how business works.

There are other considerations in this crucial matter of refining profitability. Decisions about refining capacity utilization require considerations of several types of cost distinct from the crude costs central to refining margins. Some refinery operating costs, such as workers' salaries, don't change with operating levels; they are the same whether the plant runs at 75% of capacity or at 90%. Such costs are said to be fixed. Costs that change in proportion to the amount of crude run through the refinery are said to be variable; obviously, the principal variable cost is that of crude.

When a refiner reduces plant throughput, total crude costs decline, but per-barrel crude costs do not. Producers do not base their price decisions on refinery runs, at least not directly. On what economists call a unit-cost basis therefore, variable costs do not shrink with a reduction in capacity utilization. Again, they shrink in total but not per barrel. And fixed costs on a unit basis increase when capacity utilization declines; they now are apportioned to a smaller number of barrels per day of throughput. As a result, it costs more per barrel to refine crude in a plant operating at 75% of capacity than it does in the same plant operating at a 90% utilization rate.

Because of those unit cost considerations, refiners do not like to reduce runs and capacity utilization. For physical reasons, 90% capacity utilization is about maximum. Most refiners would consider 85%–90% healthy. Anything less than about 85% is worrisome unless it results from scheduled downtime for maintenance or upgrade.

A market observer thus can tell much by examining refinery operations. Positive refining margins in excess of $3.50/bbl probably indicate a healthy refining industry. When margins begin to narrow, the observer needs to determine whether the reason is climbing crude costs, falling product prices, or both. If the reason for the pressure on margins is something that may affect the market for a while, such as economic recession, the observer should look closely at capacity utilization. Is the utilization rate near 90%? If so, refiners have room to reduce throughput without sacrificing much in the way of unit costs. If the margin pressure comes while utilization rates are 70%–75%, there will be considerably more commercial pain. In fact, developments like that often point to the need for permanent cuts in capacity, which means refinery closures.

Prices And Inflation

o discussion of oil prices is complete without some consideration of the widely misconstrued phenomenon of inflation. Rising oil prices often are credited with creating inflation. Sometimes, oil prices themselves are said to be "inflating." Neither assertion can be the case.

A rising price of a single commodity, such as crude oil, is neither inflation nor the cause of inflation. During inflation, the pur-

chasing power of money declines, which raises the prices of everything. When inflation is low or nonexistent, prices of individual
products rise and fall with demand. At least in theory, price
increases for goods enjoying demand growth should be offset by
price declines for goods with shrinking demand. When prices of a
necessity such as oil rise significantly, demand for luxuries tends to
decline and their prices, therefore, to fall. The adjustment has
nothing to do with inflation, although it might occur with inflation in progress for other reasons.

Inflation is important not just to oil price behavior but also
to economic behavior in a period of oil price change. To repeat,
rising oil prices by themselves cannot cause inflation. To the extent
oil prices constitute components of key inflation measures, such as
the consumer or wholesale price index, they might make inflation
measurements rise unless those measurements fully reflect offsetting price declines for other goods. But there is a difference
between making a needle on a gauge move and actually causing
the phenomenon the gauge is supposed to measure.

Oil prices can indirectly cause inflation, however, when monetary officials overreact to an increase in them. Central banks have
been known to raise the supply of money following oil price spurts in
an effort to cushion the shock on consumers. Unless the monetary
growth is matched by productivity gains, which it usually is not during an oil price surge, inflation results. The prices of all goods rise for
reasons other than changing supply-demand relationships for those
goods. The reason for the general price rise is an excess of dollars (or
francs or marks) relative to demand for currency.

Excessive inflation has corrosive effects on an economy, which
means it ultimately can reduce demand for petroleum. It encourages

high rates of borrowing because payoff dollars are worth less than lent dollars. Worse, it erodes capital formation by understating asset depreciation. What this means is that businesses look more profitable than they really are; invested capital recovered by depreciation, which is based on historic costs, is not sufficient to pay for replacements for worn-out equipment, which must be purchased in current dollars of diminished value. To be blamed for inflation, then, as oil price rises often are, is to be charged with a serious offense.

Inflation has another potentially perverse consequence. Inflation usually raises incomes along with the prices of goods thanks to cost of living adjustments. To the extent the adjustments match inflation, purchasing power ought to remain constant. But it usually does not because of the progressive tax structures most countries have adopted. Systems of graduated tax rates ensure that taxpayers pay more tax per dollar of income as their total incomes rise through various thresholds, or brackets. The boost inflation gives incomes, then, can never be sufficient to keep purchasing power even with generally rising costs.

This is what happened in the United States during the inflation of the late 1970s. Workers' incomes became subject to escalating tax rates as inflation pushed them into higher and higher tax brackets. Meanwhile, the phenomenon that was raising their wages and salaries also hiked prices of everything in the economy. The tax rate escalation meant purchasing power couldn't keep up with price growth. Economic growth stalled in what came to be known as "stagflation." In the United States, the inflation did not end until the Federal Reserve Bank crimped money supply growth in 1979, which created a recession that did not end until 1982. These events provide an important backdrop to oil price and demand events of the period, because at the same time the Federal Reserve was braking money supply growth, U.S. price controls had begun to phase out, and the Iranian Revolution had quadrupled crude prices.

What is important to remember is that oil prices can rise without creating inflation. And inflation can occur while oil prices are falling. Assessments of oil demand response to price changes must account for whether the price changes result from changes in supply and demand or simply from changes in the value of money.

The oil market analyst thus must account for inflationary influences in current and past markets. First, the analyst should cringe at expressions such as "inflation in the price of gasoline" (or of bread or of anything else). Inflation affects general price levels in whole economies, not individual commodities or products.

Second, comparisons of today's price with yesterday's price should account for intervening inflation. Many reports relate prices to some base year and adjust other years' prices according to inflation measures, such as the consumer price index, for each year before and since. Historic prices that have been corrected for inflation in this way are called real prices. Uncorrected prices are called nominal prices. It is common to see price or cost information reported in "constant" or "current" dollars (or francs or marks). A series of data in constant dollars has been corrected for inflation; a series in current dollars has not. Often, units are portrayed as "Millions (or thousands or hundreds) of 1982 dollars." That means the values have been corrected for inflation with 1982 as the base year.

Related to these considerations is the importance of the value of the U.S. dollar to oil trade. Oil transactions worldwide are denominated in dollars. And the value of the dollar, like those of all currencies except those of centrally planned economies, is determined by international currency trading. When the dollar is weak against, say, the Japanese yen, crude oil producers who spend a lot of money in Japan suffer. A weak dollar thus influences their trading behavior. The dollar can be weak on international markets for reasons other than inflation in the United States; however, there is no doubt that it will be weak when there is inflation in the United States. Correspondingly, if the dollar remains weak on international markets for an extended period, the United States eventually will suffer inflation—which is, by definition, a slump in the currency's purchasing power.

The degree of inflation in important trading economies as well as the state of international currency markets thus play crucial roles in the condition of oil markets. Analysts must examine oil supply, demand, and—especially—price against the backdrop of inflation trends and currency exchange rates.

INTERACTIONS OF PRICE, SUPPLY, AND DEMAND

o say that price determination in the oil market is a dynamic process is an understatement. Supply, demand, and price constantly push and pull at one another as the result of millions of producers, processors, traders, and consumers making decisions they deem to be in their best economic interests.

Price is both a product of this process and a key factor in the outcome. Like supply and demand, it cannot be viewed in isolation. Nor can it or any of the other fundamental market forces be assumed ever to hold still while the others are examined.

Price determines whether consumers consume: Whenever it rises, marginal consumers quit consuming, either by conserving temporarily or by finding a less costly alternative. When prices fall, consumers use more.

Price determines whether producers produce; falling prices persuade economically marginal producers and refiners to reduce capacity utilization or make permanent capacity cuts. Rising prices make investments in new capacity look attractive.

Eventually, the price response to changes in supply and demand affects supply and demand. No adjustment lasts forever.

T ECHNICAL
V S.
F UNDAMENTAL
A NALYSIS

The interactions of price, supply, and demand—the focus of this book—make up the essence of what is called fundamental analysis. Another way of looking at price that often appears in market reports is called technical analysis. At the core of technical analysis, which assumes that price movements form patterns that repeat themselves over time, lie charts. A key premise is that the market has responded to all possible influences by the time it has signaled the response through price.

Purely technical traders base their decisions on price trends instead of on factors that might influence supply and demand; that is, they buy and sell the market. They scour price charts for signs of "support," where buying pressure outweighs selling pressure, or the reverse, called "resistance." A sign of support may be a bottom price in a down price cycle—a "trough"—higher than the preceding trough, especially if trading is active in the latest upturn. Resistance can appear as a peak lower than its predecessor in active trading.

Technical analysis is fascinating, much more sophisticated than the simple description offered here, and important. Satisfactory treatment of the subject is beyond the scope of this book. Market watchers should at least know what analysts mean when they say things like, "The technicals look good for a price increase," or, "The price slump isn't justified by the fundamentals." They also should recognize that some measure of oil trading occurs for purely technical reasons; that is, it is motivated exclusively by price movement patterns on the assumption that the movements inherently reflect everything knowable about supply and demand. The very existence of technical trading and analysis testifies to the crucial interplay of supply, demand, and price.

While individual analysts or traders may adhere exclusively to one view of price at the exclusion of the other, there is no reason for the market observer to see fundamental and technical analysis as competing schools of thought. They are, in fact, just different approaches to a complex subject. Oil companies and traders often rely on both fundamentals and technicals on the assumption that

failure of one to show a market change signaled by the other provides reason to doubt the change amounts to the start of a real
trend.

THE
CHALLENGES
OF
KEEPING
TRACK

The market observer should understand the different
ways of analyzing price as well as the various types of
crude and product prices that appear in news and
trade publication reports. The observer needs to
know where to find information on supply and demand. And the
observer needs to understand how economic forces affecting the
crude and product markets converge in basic measures of refining
profitability.

That is how we answer the third basic question of market
analysis: How do questions about supply and demand affect, and
how are they affected by, price?

To repeat the assertion of Chapter 1, the market works. The
observer needs to understand how it works and where to find the
representative numbers.

CHAPTER FIVE

THE NONRENEWABLE, INEXHAUSTIBLE SUPPLY

The first four chapters stressed the enveloping nature of the petroleum market's essential steps. In the sense of the market as a containment system, oil at every stage must be subject to physical limits. At the surface, this process of containment incorporates physical equipment in which someone has invested money: pumping units, tanks, refinery stills, pipelines, and so forth. The handling limits of all this equipment constitute capacities, maximum extremes of which keep the system closed.

A natural containment system exists as well. It is Earth itself. Crude oil occurs in nature, usually—but not always—underground. The natural containment system has limits like those of human origin, not least of which is the volume of unproduced oil in place. For all rea-

Sophisticated seismic technology provides an increasingly clear portrayal of the underground, which helps the oil industry identify rock formations likely to hold crude oil and natural gas. The 230-ft Western Pride seismic survey vessel can tow as many as four fiber optic cables, which collect data from thousands of feet below the ocean floor. Advancing technology is one very important way oil reserves "grow." Photo courtesy of Western Atlas International.

sonable purposes, that volume must be some finite number. To be sure, nature generates oil now as it always has. But the rate at which humans extract oil from the underground greatly exceeds the rate at which nature can replace it. Given that extreme disparity between production and natural generation, oil is indeed a depleting resource, a nonrenewable supply. We are using it up.

We will never, however, run out. For physical and economic reasons, we will never extract the last drop of nature's original endowment of petroleum. This relates partly to a grand paradox of natural-resource economics. It applies to all minerals, and it plays havoc with intuition, which seldom takes adequate account of economics.

Intuition says that a finite substance that exists in quantity X and that is extracted from its natural habitat at the rate of Y per year must cease to exist in the number of years represented by X divided by Y. But economics will not permit things to work out that way. Economics wants a value for X. If not all of X can be physically measured, economics seeks a value relative to measurable parameters such as cost, price, amounts known to exist, and probabilities of further occurrence. The value of economic X, in other words, is always a function of these measurable parameters. Measurable, economic X is much more meaningful than intuitive X, about which all we know is that it is some finite quantity larger than economic X.

Being an economic creature, X follows the law of supply and demand. So does Y. Depending on the parameters by which it is evaluated, X can rise as well as fall, which distinguishes it from the intuitive, finite X. Each year, intuitive X diminishes by quantity Y, yet if Y is strong relative to economic X, prices rise because of the law of supply and demand, and economic X grows. So intuitive X shrinks while economic X grows. That is the paradox of "finite" resources.

Petroleum, like all other finite resources, has an economic X and an intuitive X and a huge range in between. Some of the petroleum above economic X may be known to exist but may not count as economic X due to other factors such as cost. The existence of this known, physical supply above and beyond economic X has powerful implications for the future of quantity X. When economic X shrinks due to extraction to the point that it constrains demand (Y), shortage exists, and prices of X rise. As a result, some portion of that physical supply beyond X begins to look economically attractive. To the extent that someone responds to the incentive, as someone inevitably will, X increases, gaining back through resource development some or all of what it lost via extraction.

So, yes, petroleum is a finite substance. But thinking of it that way can be misleading. As long as it remains impossible to determine how finite the petroleum resource is, the best approach will be to define supply economically and to realize that measuring time until exhaustion by dividing by yearly consumption produces answers devoid of meaning. In the case of petroleum, that point of exhaustion exists somewhere beyond the limits of human imagination.

RESOURCES AND RESERVES

 ntuitions of steadily approaching scarcity are nowhere more misleading than they are in the case of petroleum. Because of the nature of the substance and the size of the numbers involved, estimating either economic or intuitive quantity X for petroleum is no easy chore. To make matters worse, companies and countries disagree over what to call X once they have arrived at some reasonable guess about its size.

The problems of measuring quantities of oil in the ground should be obvious. As we have seen, the physical qualities of crude oil—density, viscosity, chemical composition—vary greatly. So do characteristics of the rocks in which oil occurs. And those oil-bearing rocks are widely dispersed across and through the planet's surface and cross section and are increasingly difficult to find.

What is more, rocks yield oil at widely disparate rates. No reservoir gives up all that it holds. On worldwide average, producers historically have left behind two-thirds of the amount of oil that they discover, although the proportion that ultimately can be produced—the recovery rate—varies from field to field. And technological advances steadily improve overall recovery rates. These characteristics of petroleum and its natural habitat, combined with uncertainties about future technology, make measurements of underground quantities of the substance challenging in the extreme.

There are two general types of these measurements: resources and reserves. On that much, most authorities largely agree.

The resource is the amount of oil the world originally contained. It is often called the resource base. The remaining resource is the resource less all that has been produced so far. By nature, the resource figure can be nothing more than a calculated estimate because a major part of it represents oil not yet discovered.

Science and experience, however, have taught us what types of rocks can contain oil and how those rocks are distributed across and within the planet. And they have provided information to help experts determine the probabilities not only of occurrence of those types of rocks but also of their containing fluid hydrocarbons.

We know, for example, that five things must have happened underground in the past for there to be oil in place now. There must have been a source rock, where the oil formed. A reservoir rock must have come into communication with the source rock because it is there, in the reservoir, that the oil resides now. A seal, usually an impermeable rock, must have come into contact with the reservoir rock to keep naturally migratory oil from traveling further. There must be a trap, the underground arrangement of reservoirs and seals that holds the oil in place. And all these things must have happened in proper order.

Experts can use knowledge of geologic history to calculate the probabilities of these events' having come together fortuitously with regard to the generation and entrapment of petroleum. Information from discoveries and geophysical studies sharpens the picture. From all this comes an evaluation of the undiscovered resource segment of the total resource number, the other segments being cumulative production to date and remaining reserves.

The distinguishing characteristic of the resource estimate is that it does not represent physical oil supply. Unless it is qualified as "remaining resource," it includes oil already produced, which of course does not represent supply, as well as reserves and a most-likely estimate of oil yet to be discovered. It thus represents a probability of oil occurrence, usually overlain by an estimate of how much might be recoverable. Indeed, some resource reports bracket the estimates with probabilities; that is, the estimates represent a range between a high-probability low value and low-probability upper extreme. A resource number includes crude oil actually discovered but goes well beyond that figure to include crude that probably exists but has not been shown to do so.

Reserves figures represent estimates of the quantities of real, producible oil in the ground. A number of categories exist for reserves, and the categories and definitions vary country by country and, to some extent, jurisdiction by jurisdiction.

In general, the term "reserves" refers to oil that is known with reasonable certainty to exist and that can be produced at sufficient profit with available technology under prevailing economic conditions. Much more must be said about resources and reserves, especially the latter. What must be emphasized here is the distinction between the terms. The resource is a broad estimate, largely based on probabilities, of all oil in the ground. Reserves are estimates, largely based on actual discoveries, of oil in the ground that can be produced with current technology at current costs and prices. Reserves constitute part of the resource; the resource refers to something much more than reserves.

THE
RESERVES
PUZZLE

o confuse things further, there are perplexing subcategories of reserves. U.S. analysts often distinguish between proved, probable, and possible reserves. In the "proved" category are those reserves that have been demonstrated through drilling to exist. Financial reports often divide proved reserves into developed and undeveloped sub-categories. Proved, developed reserves have production wells and equipment in place; their undeveloped brethren do not.

Existence is less certain for probable and possible reserves. In the "probable" category are reserves likely to be proved through subsequent drilling around existing discoveries. "Possible" reserves are volumes not yet indicated to exist but likely to be added to the proved reserves total as more is learned about the reservoir and its producing performance.

Some countries do things differently. The old Soviet Union, for example, estimated "explored" and "preliminarily evaluated" reserves, correlating to U.S. proved and probable categories. Then there were "potential resources," including those said to be "prospective" and others "predicted."[1] Still other countries have different classification schemes altogether.

Worldwide reserves estimates usually involve some combination of proved, probable, and possible reserves—what the U.S. Geological Survey calls "identified" reserves. This is probably the most useful category, because many reports of what are called proved reserves actually include probable and possible reserves as well. This is especially so with country-wide reserves estimates made by state-owned oil companies, which tend not to be as conservative as private companies in what they consider to be proved. For the analyst, the best research strategy is to seek solid estimates of proved reserves but to recognize that identified reserves inevitably creep into the totals—especially those covering whole countries or the world.

Classification discrepancies thus make for imprecision in worldwide estimates of petroleum reserves. And reserves measurement itself is no exact science. Country-wide reserves estimates are really totals of the estimates for individual fields. Making those estimates is difficult business. The fact is that a field's reserves estimate usually changes dramatically over the course of its life.

A company usually estimates reserves for a field soon after the discovery. It tests production rates, estimates reservoir volume and pressures, runs logs to measure other characteristics, and drills appraisal wells. From this first gush of information it makes a reserves estimate. Then it drills development wells and learns more about the reservoir. At some point it might try to inject natural gas or water into the reservoir to improve oil recovery rates. And it learns even more.

This education might show that the reservoir is thicker or thinner in places than the company originally thought. It might respond better to waterflooding than was predicted—or not. Later, the reservoir might be found to be amenable to more exotic recovery methods such as carbon dioxide or polymer flooding, which are called enhanced recovery methods. If so, more of the oil becomes ultimately recoverable, which means the field has greater reserves than the company originally estimated for it. In fact, this phenomenon of so-called "reserves growth" or "field growth" is the norm.

A good and important example of reserves growth is Prudhoe Bay oil field on Alaska's North Slope. The field's reserves were first added to total U.S. reserves in 1970 at 9.6 billion bbl. By any standard, that is a huge volume of oil. It represented 30% of the U.S. reserves total of the preceding year. In the next 22 years, however, Prudhoe Bay reserves "grew" by more than 2.4 billion bbl as field operators drilled more wells, installed more gas injection equipment, and learned more about the prolific Sadlerochit reservoir. That addition to reserves would qualify as a "supergiant" field if added by way of a separate discovery.

While most fields ultimately outproduce their initial reserves estimates, there are plenty of disappointments: fields in which something shows up to render the original estimate optimistic. Overall, the accuracy of reserves estimates is always some function of field age.

What is more, reserves estimates vary according to who makes them. The U.S. Securities and Exchange Commission learned that lesson during the late 1970s, when it experimented with something called "reserves recognition accounting." The SEC considered it troubling that the most significant event in an oil-producing company's existence—the discovery of oil—appeared nowhere in the company's balance sheet or income statement. Under normal accounting, the company books only its development costs for the field, then writes them down via cost or statutory depletion methods at rates corresponding to production. Thus, the SEC worried, a successful exploration company might report financial results similar to a competitor that had found nothing for years but that was living off production from past triumphs.

SEC had a very strong point. Under its proposed reserves recognition accounting, therefore, a company would estimate reserves of a discovery, project production rates and cash flows, make some assumptions about oil prices, and discount the results on the basis of an assumed 10% per year cost of capital to produce a present value of the future revenue stream. That, in essence, is how oil companies evaluate projects and properties for their own decisions.

What SEC learned, however, is that no two oil companies, not even any two petroleum engineers, arrive at the same present value for the same discovery. A major variable is that fundamental number: The original reserves estimate, generation of which is as much art as it is science. SEC decided the process involved too much subjectivity to function as a basis for financial reporting. It did, however, require public companies to make unaudited disclosures of their reserves, which has added volumes to the universe of useful oil industry data.

What smart investors have learned is what oil market observers must understand about reserves: The numbers do not represent absolute truths. The underground yields its secrets grudgingly and often with great surprise. Reserves numbers are important to the oil market insofar as they provide the foundation for production capacity; they also are very imprecise.

Imprecision does not render reserves data meaningless, however. When Saudi Arabia reports reserves of 260 billion bbl and Iran 90 billion bbl, it is useful to know that Saudi Arabia probably is understating its figure and Iran the reverse. Nevertheless, the broad meaning of the comparative figures is valid: Saudi Arabia indeed possesses on the order of three times the reserves of Iran. And Iran, in turn, probably possesses three times more technically producible oil than the United States does. The distinction here is that U.S. reserves of 26 billion bbl are nearly all proved and developed, while the Iranian figure represents a significant volume of undeveloped reserves and probably a great deal of what the United States would call "identified" reserves as well. Those subtleties do not detract from the widely accepted supposition that Iran has reserves sufficient to make it an important oil producer for many decades.

There are, then, great discrepancies in how individual companies estimate reserves for specific fields and how individual countries account for their national figures. Market observers must recognize the variability of the data and definitions but not be daunted by it.

So where do the data appear? The most frequently cited source of worldwide reserves information probably is *Oil & Gas Journal*'s annual *Worldwide Production Report,* which always appears in the weekly magazine's last issue of the year. The weakness of the *Journal*'s estimate is its reliance upon a survey for the information; it publishes what national authorities tell it about reserves, and sometimes those authorities exaggerate or tell it nothing. On the other hand, the *Journal* has extensive sources for both the survey and cross-checks, and acceptance of its report as the standard reference for reserves provides access to numbers unattainable by other sources.

REVISING
AND
EXTENDING
THE
NUMBERS

 look at how the U.S. reports reserves demonstrates the derivative nature of this numerical exercise. A word of caution, however: Through 1979, American Petroleum Institute was the standard source of U.S.

reserves information. In 1980, the federal Energy Information Administration took over the job and imposed slightly different procedures and reporting formats.

EIA begins with the prior year's reserves figure and adds and subtracts to arrive at a number for the current year. The first change is "net adjustments," which essentially corrects errors from the prior year's number. Then come "revisions" in two categories, increases and decreases. Revisions reflect new information about reservoirs and recovery rates. When a company decides it can recover 100,000 bbl more oil than it originally estimated by adding two water injection wells, that 100,000 bbl increases reserves and amounts to a revision. Revisions also include changes companies make in their reserves estimates due to significant swings in oil prices. EIA blends the adjustments and revisions into a net figure then begins accounting for changes resulting more directly from operations.

The first such figure is "extensions to old reservoirs." It includes reserves added by way of "step-out" drilling, which involves wells drilled on the periphery of known oil fields to determine whether the reservoirs have greater area than originally believed. Next come "new field discoveries," the result of successful exploration, and "new reservoirs in old fields," another exploratory triumph. Extensions, new field discoveries, and new reservoirs add up to total discoveries. From the total of discoveries plus adjustments and revisions must be subtracted the prior year's production, which of course drains from the reserves base as discoveries and other activities add to it. The remainder is the new reserves figure.

Not all countries go through the same drill in estimating

reserves, and few make it as public as the United States does. But the process illustrates several aspects of reserves estimation that observers must take into account.

First, additions to and deletions from reserves occur continuously. It is like a tub with both the drain and spigot open. If more enters the tub from the spigot than the drain sluices away, the level in the tub rises. Similarly, if positive adjustments and discoveries exceed negative adjustments plus production, reserves rise. If the drain (negative adjustments and revisions plus production) works faster than the spigot (positive adjustments plus discoveries) reserves fall.

Second, revisions account for a significant proportion of reserves additions in the United States. During the 1980s, net revisions accounted for 38.3% of the decade's total additions to reserves (Table 5–1). In fact, the strong contribution from revisions during the period led some observers in the oil industry to suspect companies of exaggerating their reserves holdings. The decade was not just a drilling bust after 1982 but also a period of active sales of producing properties.

There may indeed have been some book-cooking during the period. Given the subjectivity inherent in reserves estimation, there is certainly room for a company newly motivated by marketing to be less conservative with reserves data than before and to be so with total legitimacy. But there is a better explanation for the growing significance of revisions in U.S. reserves totals— an explanation significant to market observers for reserves everywhere.

The explanation is technology. Oil price slumps of the 1980s revolutionized oil company thinking about adding reserves. No

TABLE 5–1
THE CONTRIBUTION OF NET REVISIONS TO
U.S. RESERVES ADDITIONS

Year	Net revisions	Total additions	Share net revisions (Percent)
	——Millions of barrels——		
1980	1,889	3,964	47.7
1981	1,271	3,450	36.8
1982	434	3,276	13.2
1983	1,511	4,196	36.0
1984	2,445	4,975	49.1
1985	1,598	4,461	35.8
1986	855	3,315	25.8
1987	2,316	4,611	50.2
1988	1,463	3,601	40.6
1989	1,333	3,627	36.8
Total	15,115	39,476	38.3

Source: Author's calculations from Energy Information Administration data published in *Energy Statistics Sourcebook*, PennWell Books, 1991.

longer able to rely on ever-rising oil prices to wash away the financial effects of errant exploration, companies began to focus on efficiency. They asked themselves how to add the most reserves per dollar of invested capital and, moreover, whether doing so was economically justified in view of expected prices for resulting production. Tough financial questions led to some sobering conclusions about exploration as companies discovered that there often were better ways to add reserves, not least among them was simply to buy them from someone else.

THE
GROWING
ROLE
OF
TECHNOLOGY

he tough questions also led to strengthened emphasis on technology as a way to contain operating costs. Coming as it did at a time of booming computer capability, this renewed attention to technology produced dramatic results. Advances in seismic and logging technology gave companies a clearer, more accurate picture of the underground and of individual reservoirs than they ever had before. Drilling technologies made it possible to target wells with ever-increasing precision. And horizontal drilling came into its own, creating whole new strategies for reservoir drainage and field development.

Technology provided companies with tremendous amounts of new information about existing fields. For example, companies learned that many of their former assumptions about reservoirs did not apply fieldwide; that is, reservoirs are not as homogeneous as once thought. In one part of a field, the rock might be less porous and less permeable than it is elsewhere. Oil, therefore, will not drain from that part of the rock as efficiently. More dramatically, there might be a once-undetected wall of impermeable rock cutting off part of the reservoir. By drilling into the sections cut off from the rest, or with lower permeabilities and porosities, the field operator can improve ultimate oil recovery. That means it can add reserves.

This is a simplification of what actually occurs, of course.

Nevertheless, drilling within producing fields to boost recovery rates—so-called infill drilling—accounted for much of what little drilling occurred during the lean years of the 1980s, especially the latter half. By itself, infill drilling is no technology of great romance. But the technologies leading to it—three-dimensional seismic, cross-hole tomography, enhanced logging, and so forth—certainly are.

In parallel with those techniques came enhanced recovery technologies such as those mentioned earlier. Companies thus know not only more about what's underground but also more about how to produce it economically.

Companies gained confidence in the high-romance technologies during the 1980s and used them to learn more than had ever before been possible about the underground. In effect, nondrilling technologies increasingly replaced drilling as a research tool as companies found them far less expensive than drilling, especially drilling dry holes. Once a company might have drilled an expensive and risky wildcat in some geologic frontier. Now it might more likely spend a tenth of the wildcat's cost shooting a three-dimensional seismic survey over a producing field and conducting a feasibility study, based on results of the survey, of an infill drilling program or carbon dioxide flood. If study results are positive, the company books new reserves, which show up in the revision increase column of the EIA reserves report. It happened often during the late 1980s. It will happen more through the 1990s. And the oil is just as real as if it had been discovered in some out-of-the way prairie hundreds of miles from existing production.

Technology influences reserves figures no less elsewhere in the world than it does in the United States. The effects in the United States are simply more apparent. The United States is the world's most mature drilling province. And its remaining exploratory frontiers—

mainly its federal offshore and prospective parts of Alaska—for political reasons cannot be leased. This focuses attention on smaller, ever-more subtle exploratory targets and on the potential for increasing reserves in existing fields. To the degree companies are successful in these pursuits, the results show up as upward revisions of reserves.

Technological advances are no less important in, say, the North Sea. But the results—reserves added by way of new knowledge and application of new drilling and production techniques—are not so great a share of total North Sea reserves additions because significant volumes are still added there via discovery. And in a booming exploratory frontier such as Yemen, big recent reserves additions result from discovery only, although the estimates themselves no doubt reflect the availability of technologies not available when reserves first were estimated for an old U.S. producer such as East Texas field.

The part of the "reserves" definition having to do with what is producible via current technology is, therefore, vitally important. A useful addition to the definition might be something like "and identifiable with current technology" to reflect what is happening in a big way in the modern petroleum industry.

RESERVES/
PRODUCTION
RATIOS

he beginning of this chapter described a formula by which intuition arrives at a theoretical point of exhaustion for finite resources. Petroleum economists employ the same intuition for oil but for different reasons. They call it the reserves/production ratio. It is an interesting and important figure. But it must be used with caution.

The reserves to production ratio, or R/P ratio, can be calculated for the world or for an individual country or field. It is simply total reserves divided by annual production from those reserves. As the formula implies, the answer is expressed in years.

What the R/P ratio does not tell is the number of years remaining until depletion. Revisions, adjustments, and discoveries create reserves even as production eliminates them. As long as total additions outrun production, reserves grow. And production, the denominator in R/P calculations, changes from year to year. The R/P ratio can increase even if reserves shrink if production falls by even more. In fact, in a mature producing area, that is often what happens.

The trap to avoid is thinking of R/P ratios as measures of time until oil runs out. If that were the case, the world's R/P ratio obviously should shrink with time. It does not. The worldwide R/P ratio has been higher in recent years than at any time since at least 1970 (Table 5–2).

The R/P ratio is best thought of not as a measure of reserves but as a measure of how rapidly a given body of reserves gives up its oil. It can be used, then, as a rough gauge of the extent of development of a field, a country, or the world—subject to great change when there are significant discoveries. Extent of development is a way of measuring a producing region's maturity.

The key to understanding R/P ratios is recognizing that reserves do not deplete at steady rates. In a typical field, production builds fairly rapidly to a peak rate during the first few months or years, remains at peak for perhaps a few years, then begins to

TABLE 5–2
RESERVES/PRODUCTION RATIOS, WORLD TOTAL

Year	Reserves	Production	R/P ratio
	——Thousands of barrels——		—Years—
1970	530,696,260	16,496,467	32.2
1971	613,386,148	17,477,477	35.1
1972	632,668,710	18,306,575	31.6
1973	666,399,420	20,021,783	33.3
1974	628,456,050	20,159,643	31.2
1975	714,647,310	19,217,724	37.2
1976	658,542,850	20,720,210	31.8
1977	640,032,490	21,623,330	29.6
1978	645,734,320	21,828,095	29.6
1979	640,911,585	22,721,250	28.2
1980	642,174,790	21,657,494	29.7
1981	651,929,712	20,448,833	31.9
1982	670,349,750	19,412,890	34.5
1983	668,262,406	19,293,279	34.6
1984	669,737,600	19,807,309	33.8
1985	699,813,400	19,551,334	35.8
1986	700,557,060	20,349,772	34.4
1987	699,778,600	20,368,350	34.4
1988	889,334,400	21,170,365	42.0
1989	907,442,751	21,774,914	41.7
1990	1,001,571,623	22,065,965	45.4

Source: Author's calculations from data published in
Energy Statistics Sourcebook, PennWell Books.

decline, usually at an accelerating rate. After a slide of a number of years' duration, production eventually flattens into some rate significantly below peak, where it might well remain for years.

A producing region therefore might have a high R/P ratio because it is fairly undeveloped; discoveries have added reserves, but development has not yet brought production to high levels.

Or it might have a high R/P ratio because most of its fields are well into their decline stage but still hold significant reserves that will take decades to drain. By contrast, a thoroughly developed, mature region would have a lower R/P ratio because production from well-drained reserves is well into its low, flat period, no longer declining by much. Because of the low rate at which a mature reservoir yields oil—which, after all, is what the R/P ratio measures—and the probability that the reservoir holds more oil than originally estimated, the R/P ratio can remain low for years beyond the indicated point of exhaustion.

The United States and United Kingdom each have an R/P ratio of less than 10 years. The R/P ratio of Saudi Arabia, by contrast, is nearly 87 years, of Abu Dhabi nearly 130 years (Table 5–3). These are extremes. In general, they contrast countries with scope for increasing production capacity, Saudi Arabia and Abu Dhabi, with others possessing no such hope in the absence of major reserves additions.

For purposes of economic analysis and planning, countries need somehow to factor their consumption into the picture. One way to do that is to compute reserves/consumption (R/C) ratios and compare them with R/P ratios.[3] A country with an R/P ratio significantly higher than its R/C ratio has different economic priorities than a country where the reverse is true; the former must pursue oil to buy in international markets while the latter must pursue markets. The United States thus has an R/C ratio of 4.4 vs. its R/P ratio of 9.8. Another country in the same predicament is India, with an R/C ratio of 14 and an R/P ratio of 25.9. The United Kingdom's ratios are equivalent at 6.2. Norway's R/C ratio of 106.9 contrasts happily with its R/P ratio of 11.2.

TABLE 5-3
R/P RATIOS FOR SELECTED COUNTRIES

Country	Est. reserves as of Jan. 1, 1992 ——Thousands	Est. production for 1991 of barrels—	R/P ratio —Years—
India	6,126,740	236,155	25.9
Indonesia	6,581,293	522,899	12.6
Brunei	1,350,000	55,224	24.4
U.K.	3,994,310	649,444	6.2
Norway	7,609,400	680,360	11.2
C.I.S.	57,000,000	3,744,900	15.2
Abu Dhabi	92,200,000	710,217	129.8
Iran	92,860,000	1,219,830	76.1
Saudi Arabia	257,842,000	2,977,560	86.6
Nigeria	17,899,820	677,914	26.4
Venezuela	59,100,000	854,574	69.2
Mexico	51,298,000	1,013,605	50.6
U.S.	26,250,000	2,690,561	9.8

Source: Author's calculations from data published in *Oil & Gas Journal*'s Worldwide Production Report, December 30, 1991.

PROVING
THE
RESOURCE

o there are reserves, and there are resources: oil thought to exist, and oil known to both exist and be recoverable. Obviously, the two relate; it is crucial to understand how.

A useful way to envision the relationship is to think of exploration as the attempt to turn resource into reserves. That, indeed, is what happens. A reminder is in order, however: Reserves remain part of the resource; discovery doesn't detract from the resource, it just gives part of the resource an important additional category. The remaining resource diminishes as reserves do, through production.

So where does the world stand in this continuous process of estimation, categorization, and depletion of the petroleum endowment?

The best assessment comes from the U.S. Geological Survey (USGS), which regularly reports on global oil and gas resources at the triennial World Petroleum Congress. According to the USGS estimate reported at the 13th WPC in Buenos Aires in 1991, the world has discovered 77% of its ultimate conventional resource.[4] That means that of the total amount of oil thought ultimately ever to have existed, the processes of exploration, development, and recovery improvements have identified more than three-fourths as probably recoverable under normal economic and technological conditions. The estimate uses identified reserves, which it defines as including proved, probable, and possible reserves. It is further estimated that of total originally identified reserves, 37% has been produced. Here are the numbers:

Ultimate recoverable resource — 2.1713 trillion bbl.

Identified reserves on January 1, 1990 — 1.0527 trillion bbl.

Cumulative production through January 1, 1990 — 629.3 billion bbl.

Original, identified reserves — 1.682 trillion bbl.

Undiscovered oil — 498.3 billion bbl.

The reserves estimate is identified reserves because that is what tends to get reported most. There is a problem in that not all identified reserves are reported; the USGS researchers think they include about 75% of the world's total. And the figures are for conventional oil only; that is, petroleum thought to be recoverable with known technology with prices in an historic range below $50/bbl.

The undiscovered oil number must be handled gently. As explained before, it is an estimate of the probability of oil's occurring underground. Technically, the number cited here is the mode of a frequency distribution of estimates spanning a 90% range of probability. It boils down to the must typical value in a range of educated best guesses about undiscovered oil. The 1991 estimate thus cites a low value of 304 billion bbl and says there is a 95% chance that undiscovered oil totals more than that amount. It cites a high value of 1.047 trillion bbl and says there is only a 5% chance for there being that much. The values come from experts using all the available geological and geophysical information that they can find. The experts estimate a range of probabilities between those low and high figures and calculate the mode, which represents the value most likely to be the real one. This complicated process is described in rough, nonstatistical terms here to demonstrate that the undiscovered oil component of resource estimates is an exercise in probabilities; by its very nature, it cannot be a measure of real oil.

These estimates have strong bearing on the answer to the middle question of petroleum economics: How much oil can (or will) the world produce? They attempt to measure the world's proximity to exhaustion of a finite resource.

FINITE
BUT
INEXHAUSTIBLE?

The trouble is, the world does not yet have a solid idea about how finite its petroleum resource might be. Just as reserves have a strong tendency to grow as their owners learn more about them, so do resources expand as people increase their knowledge about the underground through exploration, refinement of current knowledge, and development of new theories. Like reserves estimates, resource assessments do not hold still. The 1991 WPC estimate of undiscovered conventional resources (for 1990) thus reflected a 64 billion-bbl increase from the 1987 estimate (for 1986). That means the world probably has another Venezuela's worth of recoverable oil still to find, given that Venezuela's reserves now total about 60 billion bbl. Why the increase? The USGS researchers learned more in the years between the estimates, especially, they said, about potential of the West Central Arabian-Iranian and North Caspian basins.

What other West Central Arabian-Iranian and North Caspian basins does the world possess, about which the world now knows too little to include in its accounting of petroleum supply potential?

Petroleum thus adds a twist to the normal resource paradox described at the beginning of this chapter. The supply life of a finite resource should be extended by the rising prices that, according to the law of supply and demand, ought to accompany depletion. As the resource grows more scarce, its value ought to climb. As its price rises, demand ought to fall, and whatever portion of supply that was economically undevelopable before ought to become attractive to development. Price rises thus ought to moderate demand growth and add incrementally to supply, and those effects ought as well to keep price growth within economically bearable limits. Over time, real scarcity becomes the dominant force, eliminating marginal markets for the commodity and forcing remaining markets to compete for supply, bidding up the price and preserving what remains for markets with no reasonable substitutes.

That is how it ought to work with petroleum. Without question, the supply of petroleum is finite. Without question, petroleum grows more scarce with use. There is as yet no reason, however, for that increasing scarcity to be a factor in price. The reason is that the limits of the resource are not within view. Indeed, they are nowhere close to the horizon. Production capacity, not reserves, is the supply constraint with the greatest potential for immediately affecting prices.

At this stage in the Age of Petroleum, ultimate supply remains more a function of human imagination and knowledge than it is a measurable physical quantity. The phenomena of reserves growth and resource expansion described in this chapter demonstrate the ephemeral nature of our notions about the outer limits of petroleum supply. And those limits apply only to conventional oil, conventional technology, and current economic conditions.

What about the two-thirds of conventional oil known to have been originally in place that, on average, remains in the ground after reservoirs are said to be depleted? The enhanced recovery techniques mentioned earlier hold out great promise for recovering some portion of this oil, if prices ever rise enough to justify their application. How much oil is this? In the United States alone, oil in place but unrecoverable via conventional means totals about 300 billion bbl. That's more than 10 times the country's reserves, roughly equivalent to U.S. reserves and Saudi Arabian reserves combined. Nowhere near all of that oil will be recovered—ever. But it is not unreasonable to think that some portion of it will come to represent recoverable resources if oil prices rise and technological advances lower the costs of enhanced recovery techniques. The potential for significant, additional ultimate supply via enhanced oil recovery exists in every producing country. In a very real sense, the world is still just taking its first and cheapest tranche from its original endowment of conventional oil.

And then there is unconventional oil—heavy and extra-heavy oil, bitumen, and petroleum-like kerogen from shale. Production of heavy oil—defined as having API gravities between 10° and 20°—already is economic in some places. Canada produces synthetic crude oil from oil sands. And Venezuela, with one of the richest endowments in the world of heavy and extra-heavy crude, is not only producing some of its heavy crude but developing innovative ways to produce, transport, and market it. In Venezuela alone, 1.6 trillion bbl of heavy and extra-heavy crude is estimated to be in place, with 250 billion bbl of it recoverable and usable at prices of $9–$12/bbl.[5]

So, to repeat, oil exists in some finite quantity. But it is less scarce than are ideas about its efficient development and use. Indeed, the world will run out of good ideas about petroleum long before it runs out of petroleum.

One implication of this is that the nonrenewable nature of the petroleum resource has little relevance to the value of petroleum as a fuel in comparison with other fuels. It is popular to favor "renewable" energy sources over "nonrenewables" such as petroleum. The thought that we are "using up" our oil frightens those who do not realize that we can neither accurately envision the outer boundary of supply nor come close (yet) to making full use of what is known to occur in the underground.

Another implication is that at some distant point scarcity might indeed begin to play some role in the valuation and, therefore, use of petroleum. The world might indeed exhaust its supply of conventional oil and, remaining dependent upon petroleum for much of its energy needs, take a hard pass at enhanced recovery and the unconventional resources of extra-heavy oil, bitumen, and shale oil. The scarcity at that point will not be of oil per se but of conventionally recoverable oil—the easy and cheap stuff to find and produce. Prices will rise, and the hard stuff, the oil that exists in such great abundance, will become economically attractive. If politicians leave the process alone, nonoil fuels will become increasingly attractive as a natural part of the process. Eventually, as nonrenewable fuels deplete and their prices climb, renewable fuels will become economically justified and take over.

That is how the process ought to work. But it will not do so. For one thing, that point of emergent petroleum scarcity will be a long time coming for conventional oil alone. Technology will make nonoil energy supplies—including natural gas—less and less costly to produce and use, which will help them compete with oil, probably long before oil scarcity becomes a significant market factor. The scale will be small, but it will be sufficient to extend the supply life of the conventional oil resource. And politics will try to accelerate the process of fuel substitution for petroleum. The effort will create unfortunate inefficiencies, and the reasons for undertaking it will be both good and bad. Among the bad reasons will be petroleum's alleged disadvantage of nonrenewability.

Related to that implication is the one most important to anyone trying to understand petroleum markets here and now. Petroleum scarcity is only a notion, valid though it may be. It cannot be measured. It has little bearing on prices. Much more important to current markets than the growing scarcity of naturally existing crude oil is production capacity, which is more a function of investment in exploration and development than it is of reserves and resources.

Petroleum is a nonrenewable resource. But the world will not run out of it as long as humans have ideas—both good ones about making efficient and economic use of a valuable substance and bad ones about not making use of and adding value to what nature has bequeathed them.

References

1. "Russian Reserves Terminology Becoming Clearer," *Oil & Gas Journal,* October 5, 1992, pp. 102–103.

2. Author's calculations from Energy Information Administration data published in *Energy Statistics Sourcebook,* PennWell Books.

3. Ivanhoe, L.F., "Scavenger Oil Production, Reserves Ratios," *Oil & Gas Journal,* May 19, 1986, p. 81.

4. Masters, C.D., Root, David H., Attanasi, Emil D., U.S. Geological Survey, "World Resources of Crude Oil and Natural Gas," 13th World Petroleum Congress, 1991.

5. Ahlbrandt, Thomas S., "Unconventional Resources—Are They in Our Future?" Eighth V. E. McKelvey forum on Mineral and Energy Resources, 1992, Houston.

CHAPTER SIX

A
DISLOCATED
SUPPLY

A defining characteristic of the oil market is petroleum's grotesque inconvenience of location. Most of the world's crude oil exists far from the principal markets for petroleum products; increasingly, production and consumption occur in different places. Transportation, therefore, occupies a vital spot in the closed system that constitutes the market.

Ocean-going tankers provide nearly all transportation between nations for crude oil and petroleum products. They belong to a fascinating industry that functions as a crucial adjunct to the petroleum business; indeed, many large oil companies own their own shipping subsidiaries.

A petroleum market analyst does not have to be a shipping expert. As the section on refining margins in Chapter 4 showed, however, transportation rates influence the profitability of process-

Tankers link oil fields, refineries, and markets. This is a product tanker in the Houston Ship Channel.

ing operations and, ultimately, the value of crude itself. Transportation rates, like oil prices, fluctuate according to conditions within the shipping market. Among the important factors in those conditions are oil demand, of which the number of required cargo trips obviously is a function, and oil price, since ships use diesel or residual oil for fuel.

While the market analyst need not know how to pilot one of the huge vessels that ply the seaborne oil trade, nor even how to forecast demand for them, he or she certainly needs to know the basics of this segment of the oil business and stay abreast of trends within it.

DISTANT MARKETS

Calculations based on figures presented in earlier chapters reveal the dislocation of the world's petroleum supply in relation to principal markets. A valid generalization is that the Eastern Hemisphere accounts for the lion's share of petroleum reserves and production, while the Western Hemisphere consumes oil in great disproportion to its contribution to supply. The reason for the Western Hemisphere's large appetite for oil is, of course, the United States, the world's single biggest oil market. It is an interesting irony that the Western Hemisphere's potential future supply role looks better than its diminishing present contribution, based on estimates of undiscovered conventional oil (Table 6–1).[1] Furthermore, most of the world's resources of extra-heavy oil, oil sands, and shale oil are in the Western Hemisphere. As long as conventional oil dominates the market for liquid hydrocarbons, however, the Eastern Hemisphere will remain the principal supply region.

In every measure of Eastern Hemisphere petroleum supply the Middle East prevails. At the beginning of 1991, the region had 662 billion bbl of estimated reserves out of the worldwide total of roughly 1 trillion bbl. And of the Middle Eastern reserves total, countries bordering the Persian Gulf accounted for a full 98%. The Middle East's estimated 1990 production of 16.25 million B/D of crude oil—92% of it from Persian Gulf countries — was more than

---

TABLE 6–1
REGIONAL SUPPLY, CONSUMPTION COMPARISONS

Region	Consumption	Production	Reserves	Undiscovered oil
	———Share of world total (percent)———			
Middle East	5	27	67	24
Western Hemisphere	35	27	15	32
United States	25	12	3	9

Sources: Author's calculations from reserves data in *Oil & Gas Journal*, consumption data in BP *Statistical Review of World Energy*, resource data from USGS.

---

one-fourth the world's total of 60 million B/D.[2] The region's importance to worldwide supply is further illustrated by the concentration of so-called supergiant fields within it. These are fields with original reserves of 5 billion bbl or more ("giant" fields have original reserves exceeding 500 million bbl). Supergiants account for more than half of the oil discovered to date. There are only 38 of them worldwide; 26 are in the Persian Gulf region.[3]

As a market for oil products, however, the Middle East barely rates. The region's consumption in 1991 averaged only 3.1 million B/D vs. the world's total of 65.5 million B/D.[4]

Attention to consumption's tilt toward the Western Hemisphere and supply's to the Eastern Hemisphere ought not detract from the existence of strong markets in the latter region. Industrialized Europe—usually represented by European countries belonging to the Organization for Economic Cooperation and Development (OECD)—consumed an average of 13.3 million B/D in 1991. And the fastest growing market is that of Asia and

Australia (often called Australasia or Asia-Pacific) which consumed 14 million B/D of oil in 1991, a 3.9% gain on consumption of 1990.

Each of these strong market regions has production and reserves of its own. But oil must move from countries that produce in excess of their needs to those that do not produce enough. And it does so in amounts exceeding 32 million B/D—the average volume of oil moving between discrete areas in 1991 (Table 6–2). That is roughly the production averages of the Middle East and Western Hemisphere combined. And it is one-half the oil consumption rate.

THE
ROLE
OF
TANKERS

his is where tankers enter the oil market picture: moving oil from where it is produced to where it is consumed. And the inter-area movements cited in Table 6–2 do not account for tanker oil carriage within countries, such as the vital shipment of only slightly less than 2 million B/D of Alaskan North Slope crude from the Port of Valdez to California and other destinations in the U.S. Lower 48. More than 7,000 vessels carry crude oil, products, chemicals, liquid petroleum gas, and liquefied natural gas around the world.[5] More than half of this large fleet represents small ships working in intra-coastal trade. The fleet of principal interest to the oil market is the

New tankers that use U.S. ports must have double hulls under a law passed in 1990. Chevron Shipping Co. placed this double-hulled vessel, the 137,000-dwt Chevron Atlantic, in service during 1993 to carry crude oil from West Africa to the Chevron refinery in Philadelphia. Photo courtesy of Chevron Corp.

one involving roughly 3,000 larger tankers and combined carriers that carry crude oil and refined products between nations.

Most of these ships have sizes in excess of 10,000 deadweight tons (dwt). Deadweight tonnage measures a vessel's carrying capacity. It is the weight of cargo, stores, bunkers, and water aboard a ship when it is fully loaded, measured in long tons of 2,240 lb each. The measurement is the difference in weight of

TABLE 6-2
INTER-AREA OIL MOVEMENTS IN 1991

From	To										
	U.S.	Canada	Latin America	OECD Europe	Africa	Asia*	Japan	Australasia	Rest of World	Uniden- tified**	Total
						Thousand barrels per day					
U.S.		70	94	255			129	18	18	416	1,000
Canada	1,015		3	23	1	16	5			48	1,111
Latin America	2,304	96		683			159	1		177	3,421
OECD Europe	408	351	6		61	3	2	7	132	657	1,628
Middle East	1,958	94	317	3,878	368	3,357	3,298	188	353	18	13,829
North Africa	277	7		2,083	85		21		121	187	2,781
West Africa	823	62		1,058	102		12			443	2,500
East and Southern Africa					15			1	2		18
South Asia							11		56		70
Other Asia	140	1				87	957	86	76	279	1,629
Japan						52		9	4	***	66
Australasia	29	2				103	52		1	33	220
Ex-U.S.S.R.	39	11	4	1,467		127			623	52	2,283
Other Non-OECD Europe	2			77			12		3		134
China	101		5	8		185	267	2			568
Unidentified**	695	18		579	6	325			50		1,673
Total imports	7,791	712	429	10,118	638	4,255	4,925	312	1,441	2,310	32,931

*Excluding China and Japan. **Includes changes in the quantity of oil in transit, movements not otherwise shown, unidentified military use, etc. ***Less than 0.05.

Source: BP *Statistical Review of World Energy*

water displaced by a vessel when fully loaded and the water displaced when it is empty. In general, 90%–95% of a ship's deadweight tonnage represents cargo capacity. Deadweight tonnage should not be confused with registered tonnage, which measures space inside a ship's hulls and converts the volume to weight at the rate of 100 ft/ton^3. Gross registered tonnage is all of a ship's internal volume. Net registered tonnage is the internal volume of spaces designed to hold cargoes. Registered tonnage is mostly a shipbuilder's yardstick. What matters most to the oil market is how much oil ships can carry, which is best measured in deadweight tonnage.

Most ocean-going oil by far travels aboard tankers. The exception is a hybrid vessel called the combination carrier, which can carry types of cargoes in addition to oil. Multiple cargo capability reduces ballast voyages—those unprofitable trips ships make back to loading areas after they have discharged cargoes. With careful planning, a combined carrier might haul oil to a mining region, where it loads copper ore for the return leg to the oil producing area. Ore-oil (O/O) combination carriers (or combis) are designed with just such trade in mind. And there are ore-bulk-oil (OBO) ships, which can carry not just oil and ore but dry bulk cargoes such as coal and grain.[6]

For true tankers used in international trade, there are some important distinctions between those used for crude oil and those that carry refined products. For one thing, product tankers do not attain the sizes that crude carriers do. The upper size limit for product tankers is about 110,000 dwt, with the normal size range more like 20,000–50,000 dwt. In products trade, there are clean-product carriers and dirty- or black-product carriers. The difference here is the need for special coatings in the cargo tanks, which high-value products such as gasoline require to prevent contamination from rust. Lower-value products such as heating oil do not require the protection. Dirty-product carriers thus can carry crude as well as product since crude also does not require the special protection. Some especially heavy products such as asphalt require heating to accommodate loading and unloading.

Product carriers are smaller and less numerous than their crude handling counterparts because most refining centers are located near market areas, so much product transportation downstream of the refinery occurs by way of pipeline, barge, or truck. The larger end of the products tanker fleet serves the so-called entrepot refining centers—those that import crude and export product—such as Singapore as well as export refineries in the Middle East. As a rule, the amount of product transported by tanker is less than one-fifth the volume of tanker-borne crude, although this percentage can fluctuate in changing markets.

Some crude carriers are larger than 500,000 dwt, making them the largest ships afloat. Those larger than 300,000–320,000 dwt (depending on the authority) are known as ultra large crude carriers (ULCCs). Tankers with sizes between about 200,000 and 300,000 dwt are called very large crude carriers (VLCCs). These are monster ships. A typical 250,000 dwt VLCC has a length of 1,140 ft, a draft of 65 $\frac{1}{2}$ ft, and a beam of 170 ft. A 1,300-ft long, 500,000 dwt ULCC with a 95% cargo factor carries more than 3.5 million bbl of crude when fully loaded.

Tankers have grown to these extremes because of economies of scale. This economic principle holds that as factors of input in a system increase, unit costs decline. This is certainly the case for tankers. The primary nonlabor input in a tanker is, of course, steel. A large ship contains much less steel per ton of carrying capacity than a smaller counterpart. In addition, operating costs do not rise in proportion to increases in carrying capacity; for example, it does not take an appreciably larger crew to handle a 200,000 dwt tanker than it does a ship half the size. According to one estimate, the cost of building a 250,000 dwt ship on a per-ton basis is half that of a 50,000 dwt vessel. The 250,000 dwt ship's 1.75 million-bbl cargo capacity is five times the smaller ship's, but the horsepower and fuel necessary to propel it are less than twice that of the smaller vessel's. Crew requirements of both ships are about the same: 20–25 persons.[7]

Scale economies became especially important during 1967–75, when the Suez Canal was closed and Middle Eastern crude had to travel around the Cape of Good Hope to reach markets in Europe and the Western Hemisphere. Even before the canal closed, however, a VLCC—which had to use the long route because of its size—could compete with the several smaller ships hauling the same amount of crude through the canal because of scale economies.[8]

The motivation to take advantage of scale economies by building ever-larger tankers intensified in the 1960s and 1970s. In 1970–71, before the Arab oil embargo escalated crude prices, freight costs amounted to about half of the fob price of crude in the Persian Gulf. Vessel sizes skyrocketed in response to pressures to reduce these costs. In 1960, the size of the average tanker barely exceeded 20,000 dwt. By 1970 the average size had reached about 48,000 dwt. The average jumped to nearly 98,000 dwt in 1980 before sliding back to about 85,000 dwt in 1989.[9]

Despite scale economies, size has its drawbacks. The world's two main canals, Panama and Suez, cannot accommodate the largest ships, although there are plans to deepen Suez to allow passage of VLCCs. And the megaships cannot enter most of the world's ports, which means their cargoes must be transferred to smaller vessels—transshipped—or discharged at facilities offshore. This balance between physical limits and scale economies keeps the fleet well mixed in terms of vessel size.

THE
FLEET
AT
WORK

The worldwide tanker fleet of some 3,200 vessels totaled about 264 million dwt in 1992.[10] Voyage lengths of some typical shipping routes from the Middle East are 6,600 mi to Northwest Europe via the Suez Canal, 6,700 mi to Japan, and 11,900 mi to North America. Steaming speeds average about 15 knots, although some ships can make 16 knots. The 1,800-mi trip from the Caribbean to the U.S. Gulf coast takes five days; the 11,000 mi journey from Ras Tanura, Saudi Arabia, to Rotterdam via the Cape of Good Hope takes 35–45 days.

Oil companies, independent shipping firms, and governments own tankers. In 1991, 72% of the tanker fleet's deadweight tonnage belonged to independent firms, 20% to oil companies, and the rest to governments and others. The trend for oil company tanker ownership has been downward since the 1970s. In 1980, for example, oil companies owned 31% of the fleet's deadweight tonnage. Government ownership has remained fairly steady.[11]

When oil companies rely less and less on tankers that they own, they obviously must rely more and more on tankers that belong to someone else. The relationship between the oil company, or shipper, and the tanker owner is called a charter. In trade parlance, an oil company is said to "charter-in" a tanker when it enters into a relationship for the vessel's use. Companies seek to make money from their shipping operations and thus try to keep owned tanker tonnage and chartered-in tonnage at some optimum balance relative to their needs for transportation. At times, a company might own or hold under charter more tanker capacity than it needs, or it may have to redistribute its vessels to better meet future needs. In those circumstances it can charter out tonnage to competitors. When it is chartered tonnage, the process is called reletting.

In the interest of flexibility, shippers usually try to maintain a mix of long, medium, and short-term charters. They rely on the spot market, which can provide single vessels for specific voyages, for short-term and balancing needs. Brokers typically provide the specialized services necessary to match short-term shipping needs with available, suitably sized vessels in the spot market trade.

A huge consideration in the decision whether to own ships or charter them in obviously is the capital investment that ownership involves. In 1991, the price of a single-hull, 250,000-dwt tanker built in Japan reached $95 million, according to the International Association of Independent Tanker Owners (Intertanko).[12] That represents a major investment and major capital charges for any company. In combination with a late-1980s tendency of oil companies to focus on core functions (such as exploration, production, and refining), it goes a long way toward explaining the decline in the company-owned portion of the world tanker fleet.

Chartering, then, is a vital function of the tanker trade. And charters come in several varieties:

Bareboat charter. In the bareboat charter, the shipper essentially leases the boat for a specific term and provides everything else, including crew, and handles all expenses. The shipper, in other words, does everything except own (and therefore amortize the debt of) the vessel. This type of charter is also called demise charter.

Time charter. The owner retains the costs and risks of vessel operation under another lease-like arrangement called the time charter, providing the shipper a fully equipped vessel and a full crew at a certain rate per day or other period. Operating costs cover the crew, maintenance and repairs, and insurance. The shipper in a time charter pays for bunkers (fuel), cargo handling, and the use of ports and canals.

Consecutive-voyage charter. Under a consecutive voyage charter the owner agrees to make a specified number of round trips between or among designated ports with a designated vessel. The shipper pays for the service at an agreed rate per ton of cargo. The owner handles voyage and operating costs; apportionment of cargo handling costs varies from charter to charter.

Contract of affreightment. Like the consecutive voyage charter, a contract of affreightment covers a specified amount of cargo at a specified rate per ton, with the owner paying the expenses. This type of charter does not designate the vessel to be used and usually is not as oriented to round-trip voyages as the consecutive voyage charter. It provides much flexibility but requires that shippers and owners closely coordinate cargo lifting and discharge times. Owners of combination carriers obviously find contracts of affreightment especially useful.

Single-voyage charter. The single-voyage charter is like a consecutive-voyage charter—the shipper paying a rate per ton of cargo, the owner paying costs and, maybe, cargo handling fees—except that it covers only one trip.

REGISTRATION

uch ado is made in the tanker business about tanker registration and flags of registry. Tankers must be registered somewhere. Some nations register and use merchant marine fleets mostly for their own purposes and for imports and exports. They include traditional maritime countries such as France, Japan, and the United States. Another category of registering nations comprises the so-called cross-traders, which use merchant marine fleets to carry cargoes among other nations. They include Britain, Norway, and Greece. Then there are flag-of-convenience nations, which maintain ship registries to make money but have no domestic need for most of the shipping they register. The main flag-of-convenience nations are Liberia and Panama. Others include Cyprus, Singapore, and Bermuda.[13]

Registration requirements vary among the nations. In general, the national registries of maritime nations and cross traders impose taxes or operating restrictions that raise costs in ways that flag-of-convenience registries do not. It is common, therefore, for the vessels of one shipper to fly under different flags. Fleet operators try to match registration to their needs, seeking the best economics and maximum flexibility. U.S. shippers, in particular, make heavy use of flags of convenience. Ships flying the U.S. flag must be built in the United States and have American crews. Usually, U.S. labor and construction costs exceed those elsewhere so companies can save millions of dollars during the construction and operating life of a tanker by registering somewhere other than the United States. Indeed, most ships operating under the U.S. flag steam exclusively between U.S. ports, a trade reserved to them by law.

How
Much
It
Costs

hipping rates are extremely volatile. Shippers and owners must make chartering decisions based on their expectations about freight rates and the degrees to which they can tolerate the surprises that the tanker market can spring upon them.

Rates, like everything else, depend upon supply and demand. Supply and demand, in turn, vary from route to route and generally fluctuate in accordance with oil market swings. Strong demand in Northwest Europe, for example, might increase the amount of tanker capacity needed to ship crude to Rotterdam from the

Middle East. For a while, therefore, freight rates rise for that route. But if too many ships respond to the rate hike and steam for the Persian Gulf, too much capacity becomes available and rates decline. The same holds true on a global scale: Too much tanker capacity afloat in relation to shipping requirements—itself a function of oil demand—depresses rates.

Rates for single-voyage charters provide the best gauge of shipping market conditions for specific routes at any given time. They represent the spot market, reflecting demand for and supply of tanker tonnage at the margin; that is, they show what a shipper is willing to pay, and a ship owner is willing to accept, for an extra measure of transportation. Since such charters are denominated in dollars per ton of cargo, and since information on such charters is available from any number of shipping and oil industry sources, it is not difficult to learn how freight costs are affecting the oil trade.

The shipping industry, however, facilitates spot market assessment with an index for comparing basic daily revenue-generating potentials of specific voyages. The measurement is called Worldscale. Worldscale Associations in New York and London track spot rates in their assigned areas of coverage and calculate a rate, in dollars per long ton, representative of standard round trips for a hypothetical standard tanker. Calculations account for route characteristics such as canal fees and transit times and costs at the ports involved. The index values are expressed in Worldscale points. When the dollar per ton rates on two routes both are at Worldscale 100, abbreviated W100, tankers on those routes and charging those rates earn identical revenues per day—at least in theory.

Worldscale schedules, published biannually, provide a useful

TABLE 6-3
SAMPLE AVERAGE SHIPPING COSTS IN
FEBRUARY 1993

Cargo and route	Worldscale	$ per barrel
Distillate, Caribbean to New York (200,000 bbl)	203	1.15
Resid, Caribbean to Houston (380,000 bbl)	115	0.71
Resid, Caribbean to Houston (500,000 bbl)	129	0.80
Distillate, N. Europe to New York (200,000 bbl)	202	1.95
Crude, N. Europe to Houston (400,000 bbl)	122	1.58
Crude, W. Africa to Houston (910,000 bbl)	82	1.16
Crude, Persian Gulf to Houston (1.9 million bbl)	46	1.28
Crude, W. Africa to N. Europe (910,000 bbl)	85	1.00
Crude, Persian Gulf to N. Europe (1.9 million bbl)	46	1.22
Crude, Persian Gulf to Japan (1.75 million bbl)	47	0.75

Source: Drewry Shipping Consultants Ltd. data published in *Oil & Gas Journal*, March 15, 1993, p. 79.

way to assess freight economics but in no way represent real rates, or even averages of real rates. What they provide is a basis for comparison. Rates for two routes might both be $6/ton but represent W125 on one and W80 on the other. The W125 means 125% of W100, and the W80 means 80% of W100. The earning power of the route on which $6/ton represents W125 thus is significantly greater than the other (Table 6-3).

Worldscale points provide the unit of measurement for a number of market gauges. The best known among them probably is the Average Freight Rate Assessment (AFRA) calculated by the London Tanker Broker's Panel. The monthly report expresses the weighted average cost of commercially chartered tonnage in several vessel categories. Thus AFRA measurements above W100 reflect market strength, below W100 the reverse. AFRA averages are just that, averages. They include consecutive voyage and time charters during the report period, as well as spot charters fixed within the coverage dates. Thus they show market trends but cannot represent the market itself.

MARKET TRENDS

Oil market growth of 7%/year in the 1960s and the Suez Canal's closure in 1967 set up the tanker market for a bust in the 1970s and 1980s. There was nothing in sight to retard oil consumption. And, as mentioned before, the increase in long haul tanker traffic in the absence of the Suez route added to the importance of scale economies, creating a surge in construction orders for VLCCs and ULCCs.

The Arab oil embargo changed everything. What started as a deliberate trade contraction targeted at the United States and the Netherlands became a true reduction in internationally traded crude as prices rose and demand fell. The unexpected development dropped tanker rates from W240 to W80 and rendered unnecessary much of the tanker capacity on order at the time—and the order book was huge. In 1974, tankers totaling 200 million dwt were on order while the existing fleet measured 274 million dwt.[5]

The crude shipping industry took another blow later in the 1970s, when production came on stream in Alaska and the North Sea. The new production, eventually to build to 2 million B/D in Alaska and nearly 4 million B/D in the North Sea, cut deeply into the long haul crude trade. Tanker sailings from the Middle East in 1985 amounted to less than half their levels of 1977 (Table 6–4).

Reactions to the shipping crash of the 1970s and 1980s demonstrate the options fleet operators have in dealing with tanker capacity surplus. First, there is slow-steaming, in which vessels deliberately travel at speeds below design capabilities in order to conserve fuel and thereby cut bunker costs. By prolonging trips, slow-steaming has the added effect of reducing overall cargo-carrying capacity, which strengthens prices by cutting the "supply" of transportation service.

Fleet operators also reduce capacity by placing vessels in temporary storage, which is called *lay-up*. Obviously, the decision to lay up a vessel is a drastic one since the ship earns no revenue during the lay-up period. During the worst of the tanker crash following the Arab oil embargo, a number of new tankers went straight from the shipyard to lay-up. In the ultimate capacity-reduction tactic, ship owners simply sell vessels to ship-breaking companies for scrap. Business for the ship-breakers was good during the tanker bust.

The rebound came after the oil price crash of 1985–86. It was then that Saudi Arabia abandoned its single-handed strategy of defending crude prices by restricting production. Lower prices revived growth in demand for crude and, even more, for low-

TABLE 6–4
TANKER SAILINGS FROM THE MIDDLE EAST

	1977	1978	1979	1980	1981	1982	1983	1984	1985	1986	1987	1988	1989	1990
					Million deadweight tons									
Arabian Gulf	1,024.2	920.2	863.5	774.5	621.4	471.1	422.0	398.9	340.1	418.9	409.2	426.2	487.2	536.1
Red Sea East					21.9	65.8	27.9	37.6	45.1	71.2	64.5	41.9	36.5	44.4
Mediterranean	4.1	14.9	45.8	44.5	53.8	57.6	56.2	69.3	77.5	73.4	84.2	103.6	110.3	69.7
Total	1,028.3	935.1	909.3	819.0	697.1	594.5	506.1	505.8	462.7	563.5	557.9	571.7	634.0	650.2

Source: Arthur Andersen & Co., Cambridge Energy Research Associates Inc., *World Oil Trends.*

priced, long-haul crude from the Persian Gulf. Although it never reverted to the boom conditions of the period before the Arab embargo, tanker shipping enjoyed a fairly steady recovery into the early 1990s.

By the beginning of 1992, however, the tanker order book had reached 43 million dwt, highest level since 1976, and rates had collapsed once again. Toward the end of the year, Intertanko was warning that as much as 30% of the world's fleet was surplus to demand.[10]

THE
FUTURE
FOR
TANKERS

Forecasting demand for tankers is tricky business. Fleet operators must conduct the exercise, however, in order to know how many tankers they'll need.

A tanker demand forecast starts with energy and petroleum demand projections. It then tries to calculate the rates at which crude and products will have to be shipped between producing regions and major importing ports. It somehow must convert those shipping rates into numbers of tankers of some assumed size steaming at some standard speed. Tanker sizes must account for route peculiarities, such as shallow water ports and canals, that impose draft or beam limits.

The process quickly becomes complicated. The biggest problem with it, however, is the variability of key factors such as petroleum demand and shipping patterns, both of which vary as the market shifts. Because and in spite of these hazards, tanker forecasts are compiled with care. A decision to build an $80 million tanker assumes that the need for the vessel will remain valid for the two years or so required for construction and for some significant portion of the two decades it can be expected to operate. Unfortunately, all market forecasts depend to some degree on extensions of existing trends, altered in accordance with changes that can be foreseen. As the tanker market—like the oil market—learned in the 1970s and 1980s, the biggest changes have a way of being those that no one can predict.

The tanker market recovery of the late 1980s and early 1990s seemed destined to extend at least into the latter half of the decade, although no one expected another shipping boom. The main threat was the ever-present potential of a supply interruption strong enough to push prices up and demand down.

In late 1992, Drewry Shipping Consultants Ltd. of London predicted that by 1997 annual shipments would reach 1.62 billion metric tons (tonnes) of crude oil and 350 million tonnes of refined products, compared with 1.4 billion tonnes of crude and 271 million tonnes of products in 1991. Drewry foresaw a rise in shipping from the Middle East to 1.03 billion tonnes by 1997 from 801 million tonnes in 1991.[10]

The numbers themselves revealed one important trend likely to shape future shipping patterns: a greater percentage rise for seaborne movements of products than of crude. The projection reflected growth in export refining capacity in the Middle East and, to a lesser extent, Asia. Since product tankers do not attain the sizes of crude carriers, the trend pointed to an increasing number of vessels and a decreasing average vessel size.

A crucial shipping route change that could be foreseen in the early 1990s, although its timing remained uncertain, was the plan to enlarge the Suez Canal to enable it to accommodate fully laden VLCCs. Eventual completion of the expansion will effectively reduce tanker demand by the equivalent of 25 VLCCs.

A major concern of the early 1990s was a law passed in the United States in response to the March 1989 crude spill in Alaska's Prince William Sound by the Exxon Valdez. Signed into law on August 18, 1990, the Oil Pollution Act mandated major changes in tanker design and raised prospects of unlimited liability for owners of tankers involved in spills.

The redesign change required all new or retrofitted tankers entering U.S. waters and larger than 5,000 gross tons to have double hulls. Single-hulled vessels of that size were to be excluded from U.S. waters by 2010 according to a phaseout schedule based on vessel age and tonnage.

The liability provisions of the act set a limit on a shipowner's liability to the larger of $1,200 per gross ton or $10 million for vessels larger than 3,000 gross tons. Liabilities covered oil removal costs and damages, including those to natural resources, resulting from a spill. In addition, the law imposed no limit on the authority of a state or local government to create additional liabilities. This was important because some coastal governments in the United States had no liability limits at all. The act had several other provisions, including a 5¢/bbl fee on oil to pay for a standing pollution cleanup fund.

The act raised concerns in the shipping business around the world. Here the biggest oil importer in the world was making requirements that would raise the cost of new ships and, worse, would expose owners to unlimited liability in the event of mishap. The unlimited liability provision, in particular, led some major shippers to withdraw from routes bound for the United States. This did not in any way diminish tanker service to the United States. A market that large will always attract the transportation functions that it needs.

The Oil Pollution Act, in fact, was just one of a number of initiatives taken at about the same time around the world to tighten governance of tanker safety. A number of classification societies, which rule on the seaworthiness of vessels, reported withdrawals of significant numbers of vessels with owners unable or unwilling to abide by toughened new standards. There was concern at the time that some of these vessels simply sought classification from less strict societies.

There was no doubt, however, that tanker safety was receiving new emphasis in the wake of the Exxon Valdez spill. New physical and operational standards added to the complexity of a crucial part of the oil market as it headed for what nevertheless seemed to be a period of at least modest prosperity in the century's last decade.

REFERENCES:

1. Undiscovered oil estimates come from Masters, C.D., et al., USGS, "World Resources of Crude Oil and Natural Gas," World Petroleum Congress, 1991.

2. "Worldwide Look at Reserves and Production," *Oil & Gas Journal,* Dec. 30, 1991.

3. Riva, Joseph P., Jr., Congressional Research Service, "Dominant Middle East Oil Reserves Critically Important to World Supply," *Oil & Gas Journal,* Sept. 23, 1991, p. 62.

4. Consumption figures come from *BP Statistical Review of Energy,* June 1992, which measures inland demand plus international aviation and marine bunkers and refinery fuel and loss.

5. *The Shell Review,* July 1992, Royal Dutch/Shell Group.

6. Nersesian, Roy, *Ships and Shipping: A Comprehensive Guide,* PennWell Books, 1981.

7. *The Downstream: A Guide to Petroleum Refining, Marketing and Transportation,* Exxon Corp., 1986.

8. "Our Industry Petroleum," British Petroleum Co. plc, 1977.

9. "Traded Oil and Shipping Requirements," *Global Oil Report,* November–December 1991, Centre for Global Energy Studies, London.

10. "Drewry: Substandard Tankers Should be Removed from Fleet," *Oil & Gas Journal,* October 26, 1992, p. 39.

11. *World Oil Trends,* Arthur Andersen & Co. and Cambridge Energy Research Associates Inc., 1992.

12. *Oil & Gas Journal,* Newsletter, May 22, 1992.

13. *Tankers and the Flags They Fly,* Exxon Background Series, 1979, Exxon Corp.

CHAPTER SEVEN

THE
VITAL
FUNCTION
OF
OPEC

On September 17, 1992, Sixto Duran Ballen, president of Ecuador, announced that his country would withdraw from the Organization of Petroleum Exporting Countries. His reason: Ecuador received no benefits from the organization and could no longer justify the $3 million/year in dues and meeting costs and production restraints that accompanied membership.

The news inspired a new round of international speculation about OPEC's imminent disintegration. But the same speculation had arisen before. It arose when revolution replaced the Shah of

Politics inevitably enters into deliberations of the Organization of Petroleum Exporting Countries. Captions on these building paintings in Tehran read, "Obedience to Khamenei is obedience to Imam (Khomeini)." Ayatollah Khamenei succeeded Ayatollah Khomeini as leader of Iran's Islamic revolution when the latter died in June 1989.

Iran with the Ayatollah Khomeini in 1979, when Iran invaded Iraq in 1980, when OPEC reduced its official crude oil price in 1983, when Saudi Arabia crushed the market with high production in 1985 and 1986, when Iraq invaded Kuwait in 1990.

Yet OPEC survived each of those upsets. And it certainly will survive withdrawal from membership of a producer as inconsequential as Ecuador.

The reflexive and always premature declarations of OPEC's death have complex origins that say more about the people who make them than about OPEC itself. Many people in the consuming world blame OPEC for the embargo of 1973–74. Most economists dislike cartels. And, sad as it is to say, some people automatically treat with suspicion any group they associate with Arabism or Islam. Behind nearly all rumors about OPEC's death, therefore, lies some degree of wishful thinking.

Each of the assumptions underlying these antagonisms toward OPEC is flawed. OPEC did not impose the embargo. The group's purpose is not to function as a cartel; when it has tried to do so, it has failed. And it is decidedly not an Arab or Islamic group: While important members fall into one or both of those categories, others, such as Venezuela, belong to neither.

That OPEC possesses the power to influence something as important as the price of oil is, however, beyond question. It is an exclusive group. It is quintessentially political. Those characteristics represent very good reasons for the consuming world and for consuming nation governments to watch OPEC's behavior with great concern.

But OPEC does not have the power to annul market forces. In the early 1990s, not all of the group's members accepted that reality. Nor had all of its perpetual antagonists in the consuming world, who continued to insist that as long as there was an OPEC there could be no free market for oil.

In the early 1990s, however, there was much less clamoring within OPEC for ever-higher oil prices than there had been in the 1970s and 1980s—although there was some. OPEC meetings focused more on supply and demand balances than on the political agendas that dominated earlier meetings, though politics still played a role. There were still occasional calls for production cuts designed to raise prices, but they came more from members responding to genuine needs for revenues than from firebrands seeking to punish political enemies in the consuming world.

In the years since its birth in 1960, OPEC had learned more than a little about how markets work. Maybe it had learned more than the governments of key consuming nations, who in the latter period could not decide whether to fault the exporters' group for keeping prices too high in the 1970s and early 1980s or too low in the 1990s.

To repeat the maxim of Chapter 1, markets work. OPEC's growing accommodation of that reality to its politics, aided in no small part by the copious oil reserves that its members control, will belie death reports for many years. "We have the oil," Saudi Oil Minister Hisham Nazer once told a group of consuming nations during an effort to promote cooperation between consumers and producers. "You need the oil."

Oil market wisdom begins there.

EXCESS
CAPACITY
AND
OPEC'S
INFLUENCE

OPEC, indeed, has the oil—77% of the world's reserves, to be precise. In 1991, members of the producers' group accounted for 39% of the world's production, even with output severely constrained in Kuwait and Iraq. Moreover, the group's reserves-to-production ratio of 87 years was nearly twice the worldwide figure (Table 7–1). This means that OPEC's production capacity is restrained not by reserves but by the extent of development of those reserves, which is a function of investment in drilling and production equipment. OPEC usually can adjust its production and, in time, its production capacity to economic conditions. Its production represents the margin of worldwide crude oil supply. This is the reason that OPEC—or at least some group comprising the most important producers in what now is OPEC—will remain vitally important to the oil market for many years to come.

OPEC's influence over price derives not just from reserves and production but from potential output from those mammoth reserves: production capacity. The U.S. Central Intelligence Agency estimated total OPEC maximum sustainable capacity in mid-1992 at 25.15 million B/D. This is the most that members can produce on a prolonged basis without straining equipment or damaging reservoirs. The CIA estimated available production

TABLE 7-1
OPEC RESERVES, PRODUCTION, R/P RATIOS

	Reserves, end 1991 (Billions of barrels)	Production, 1991 (1,000 B/D)	R/P ratio, 1991 (Years)
Iraq*	100.0	230	100+
Iran	92.9	3,260	78.2
Kuwait**	94.0	90	100+
Saudi Arabia	257.8	8,580	83.6
Venezuela	59.1	2,645	63.9
Qatar	3.7	440	23.8
Libya	22.8	1,510	41.7
Indonesia	6.6	1,515	12.2
U.A.E.	98.1	2,620	100+
Algeria	9.2	1,310	21.2
Nigeria	17.9	1,895	26.0
Ecuador	1.6	315	13.4
Gabon	0.7	295	6.8
Neutral Zone	5.0	130	100+
Total	769.4 (76.9% of world total)	24,835 (38.6% of world total)	86.6 (vs. 43.4 for total world)

*Production restrained by United Nations export embargoes.
**Production severely cut by damage to oilfield facilities during Iraqi occupation.

Source: BP *Statistical Review of World Energy,* June 1992.

capacity—the most that the members could produce on short notice for 90 days—at 25.75 million B/D (Table 7–2).

These totals exclude production capacities of Iraq, which in mid-1992 remained subject to an export embargo, and Kuwait, which was restoring capacity eliminated by Iraq in 1990 and 1991. Before the Persian Gulf conflict, Kuwait had production capacity approaching 2 million B/D, Iraq about 3.5 million B/D.

Capacity estimates must be interpreted with caution. Many OPEC countries, especially those around the Persian Gulf, never publish capacity figures. In the lavishly oil-endowed countries around the gulf, production capacity is limited not by reserves but by past investment in development drilling and production equipment, as well as that equipment's current state. At any given time, it is difficult for outsiders to estimate the condition and capability of facilities such as gas/oil separators, water injectors, compressors, pipelines, and similar gear.

Saudi Arabia, for example, surprised everyone with its production response to the Iraqi invasion of Kuwait in 1990. In the early 1980s Saudi production capacity, at least the available rate, was thought to be about 10 million B/D. The country had produced that much on a surge basis to make up for supply losses accompanying the Iranian Revolution of 1978 and 1979. But during the market weakness of the mid-1980s, Saudi Arabian Oil Company (Aramco) had "mothballed" much producing equipment no longer necessary to meet demand for Saudi oil. The country's production capacity was thought to have fallen to about 6 million B/D, and no one knew how much of the deliberately idled capacity could be restored quickly. The test came in the Iraq-Kuwait crisis. Within six months, Saudi Arabia was producing 8.5

TABLE 7–2
OPEC PRODUCTION CAPACITIES

	Available capacity, mid-1992	Maximum sustainable capacity, mid-1992
	———1,000 B/D———	
Iraq	—	—
Iran	3,400	3,000
Kuwait	—	—
Saudi Arabia	8,500	8,500
Venezuela	2,500	2,400
Qatar	600	600
Libya	1,500	1,500
Indonesia	1,300	1,300
U.A.E.	2,210	2,210
Algeria	800	800
Nigeria	1,800	1,700
Ecuador	330	330
Gabon	300	300
Neutral Zone	300	300
	23,540	22,940

Notes: Available capacity reflects the most a country can produce for 90 days from existing facilities, although output on a given day might exceed this level. Maximum sustainable capacity is the peak rate sustainable for one year with prudent facilities operation and reservoir maintenance. Absence of data from Kuwait and Iraq results from facilities damage and uncertainties following the Persian Gulf War. Ecuador withdrew from OPEC at the end of 1992.

Source: U.S. Central Intelligence Agency data.

million B/D. Oil companies were astonished; privately, some predicted the Saudis could not keep production above 8 million B/D through the war year of 1991 due to limitations in water injection capability. Yet average Saudi production remained above 8 million B/D not only through 1991 but through 1992 as well and showed no sign of slowing down. Aramco accomplished the capacity surge with an impressive mobilization of personnel, capital, and equipment in an effort that, among other things, validated the costly care with which redundant equipment had been physically idled during the 1980s.

Flexibility thus is an important characteristic of capacity where reserves do not function as a limit. OPEC's high reserves-to-production ratio means there is much flexibility in the upward direction. As Chapter 5 noted, R/P ratios do not really measure time remaining until reserves depletion; rather, they indicate rates at which reserves are yielding their bounty. The higher the R/P ratio, the greater the scope for additional development and commensurate additions to production capacity. Iraq, Kuwait, the United Arab Emirates, and the Neutral Zone shared by Kuwait and Saudi Arabia all have R/P ratios of more than a century.

So OPEC—or its successors, which doubtless will include the high R/P ratio members of the present organization—will retain market influence as long as it controls so much of the world's production capacity. It is production capacity that answers much of the critical market question of Chapter 1: How much oil can or will the world produce?

ANSWERING THE SUPPLY QUESTION

OPEC occupies its position of principal market influence because it controls enough production capacity to provide a significant answer to the oil supply question. Just as the market always has marginal consumers—those ready to begin or quit buying oil in response to any change in price—it has a marginal supplier as well. And OPEC is it. Nature, economics, and history have conspired to make this so.

The market, it must be remembered, demands a certain surplus of capacity at all stages of the closed system that conveys petroleum from the underground to market. This demand results from concern by oil sellers and resellers all along the chain of production, processing, and transportation activities for replacement supply. The concern applies no less to production capacity than it does to processing, storage, and transportation capacity—and perhaps, in view of the politics of oil production, even more so.

Yet who will spend the money to explore for oil, develop reserves, and install hardware just to produce nothing and generate no revenue until the market beckons? The question is as old as the oil industry, which makes it older than OPEC. It falls to OPEC members to grapple among themselves for an answer because they possess nearly all of the spare capacity that the market demands. This is the core of the group's influence over price. If it can limit production sufficiently, relative to demand, it can drive up the price of crude oil worldwide. By producing "too much," it can drive the price down.

In those simplistic terms, OPEC's role in the market might seem like a capricious one. Indeed, to some observers it is. But the role evolved for sound economic reasons. Not only does OPEC control a disproportionate share of the world's reserves and production capacity, but it represents the world's cheapest production capacity as well. Technical production costs in at least parts of Saudi Arabia, Kuwait, and perhaps the United Arab Emirates are said to fall below \$1/bbl. Production in the North Sea costs perhaps \$10/bbl. In the United States, much production costs \$12–\$15/bbl.

This is an extremely broad cost spectrum. It gives low cost producers with spare capacity powerful leverage. When the oil price is \$15/bbl, some high-cost producers barely break even, yet \$2/bbl producers enjoy huge profit margins. In such conditions, a low-cost producer with spare capacity can (and often does) find it advantageous to increase production, weaken prices, and make up for the shrunken profit margin with increased volume and market share. The market share gain, of course, comes at the expense of the high-cost operator producing at the margin of profitability. To that producer (now, perhaps, a former producer), the process no doubt seems like caprice. To the low-cost producer it is nothing more than the rational exercise of what economists call comparative advantage.

OPEC thus controls virtually all of the world's spare production capacity and enjoys a huge cost advantage that gives it broad discretion in the deployment of its producing ability. It is discretion that enables OPEC to influence worldwide oil supply and, therefore, price.

The group's success in exerting that influence is spotty, at best, for reasons that will become clear. And on those occasions when the group does manage to hold prices at its target level, the rest of the world forever argues about whether that level is the right price. OPEC comes in for special criticism when its actions seem to keep prices above the consensus marginal cost of production. According to economic theory, a commodity's price should approximate its marginal cost of production; that is, the cost incurred by the producer who would lose money if the price dropped from its current level. The amount by which prices exceed the marginal cost of production is deemed to represent "economic rent." According to theory, economic rent cannot endure; the high profits that it represents act as a lure to competition, which generates new supply and suppresses price.

The theory will receive no argument here. Its usefulness as a real-time analytical tool, however, will—later in this chapter. What must be stressed at this point is something so obvious that it can be all too easy to forget: OPEC members above all base their oil production and pricing decisions on what they consider to be their own best economic interests, notwithstanding the high-minded communiqués that usually follow their meetings. It is against this standard that OPEC behavior can be most accurately assessed, whether or not the group's decisions result in prices that comport with what outsiders say the price ought to be. When OPEC ministers err on production and price, as they often do, the market punishes their misbehavior quickly enough. The worst mistake that can be made about OPEC is to think that its pricing decisions possess some magical immunity against the stern law of supply and demand.

AN
INHERITED
ROLE

OPEC's role, then, is to balance the market, to utilize enough of its production capacity to satisfy demand. Within that role it has room to exercise discretion. Demand, after all, responds to price, and by manipulating supply, OPEC certainly can influence price. The role, however, has mostly to do with balancing the market. And OPEC did not invent the job; it inherited it.

The oil market's preference for surplus capacity preceded OPEC's existence by many years. This means some other entity must have apportioned idle producing power and wielded the associated influence over price in the prior years. Indeed, before OPEC, a complex network of oil company agreements, production controls, and—later—import restrictions performed the task.

The network operated on two fronts: the United States, which until World War II was not only the world's biggest petroleum market but also its major oil exporter, and the Middle East, which established its position as a potentially low-cost, high-volume supplier as early as the late 1920s. Before OPEC's ascendancy, the network generally attempted to balance supplies from these two great producing regions so as to protect American producing interests yet keep prices low enough to suit refiners and promote demand growth. This was possible because international oil companies controlled the Middle East's immense reserves and because the companies based in the United States possessed strong influence in Washington, D.C., and the capitals of Texas, Oklahoma, and Kansas.

Middle Eastern market controls took shape with what became known as the "Red Line Agreement," which reorganized the old Turkish Petroleum Company into Iraq Petroleum Company, owned by a group of American and European oil companies. Under the 1928 agreement, none of the companies could develop concessions in what was essentially the old Ottoman Empire except through Iraq Petroleum. This provided an indirect control of supply by limiting exploration and development within the affected region and even outside the area, particularly in Iran and Kuwait, by way of ownership links. An important exception to the Red Line Agreement was Saudi Arabia, where Standard Oil Company of California acquired a concession and formed Arabian American Oil Company with Texaco in 1933. Neither company was a signatory to the Red Line Agreement.[1]

Later in 1928, officials of Royal Dutch/Shell, Standard of New Jersey, and Anglo-Persian Oil (British Petroleum) signed the "As-Is Agreement" during a meeting at Achnacarry Castle in Scotland. They essentially agreed to refrain from competing with one another for market share, to share facilities and expand only in line with market demand, and to restrict broad price effects of isolated surpluses. Other companies joined the agreement, which broadened in scope to set sales quotas, fix prices, and accommodate buyouts of nonsignatories.

The Achnacarry pact operated in relative secrecy until release in the U.S. Congress of a report on its details in 1952. The report's ominous but not inaccurate title: "The International Petroleum Cartel."[2]

These agreements, in parallel with agreements among companies not to compete technologically in certain areas, certainly contradicted antitrust sentiments, if not laws, in the United States. They nevertheless served a vital function: They helped to manage a production capacity surplus that otherwise would have kept the market in constant disarray and impeded the orderly development of distribution systems and technologies. Furthermore, they did not work very well. Discovery and development of Saudi Arabia's huge reserves, as the world has seen, proceeded nicely.

The United States faced runaway surplus at the same time. Discovery in 1930 of giant East Texas oil field made so much oil available that prices sank to 25¢/bbl from more than $1 within two years. Competition among producers became violent. It fell to the governors of Oklahoma and Texas to manage the surplus production capacity: They dispatched national guard troops to shut down oil fields.

Late in 1932, the Texas legislature passed a law that became the cornerstone of official U.S. production restraint. The law broadened an existing state function called prorationing to account for market demand. Prorationing is the restraint of output by all producers in proportion to their abilities to produce. The Texas Railroad Commission had responsibility for the function, assigning producers their production "allowables." Before the market demand legislation, the commission based its prorationing decisions on conservation; that is, it based production constraints on reservoir management considerations that producers would ignore in periods of heavy competition—meaning most of the time. By preventing overproduction, state prorationing was deemed to prevent the waste represented by otherwise producible oil left in prematurely depressurized reservoirs.

The step from conservation-based prorationing to market demand prorationing was a large one. It put the Texas Railroad Commission, and subsequently the commission's counterparts in other key producing states, in the business of managing surplus production capacity for the sake of price.

Like most systems of price management, prorationing suffered from the diversity of interests among those subject to it. In this period from 1930 through World War II, oil companies were far from united in what they wanted from the supply and price management scheme. Integrated companies with Middle Eastern producing interests liked cheap feedstock for their refineries, while independent producers in Texas and Oklahoma viewed the low-cost foreign crude as a threat to their pricing structure. Governments of the Middle Eastern countries, meanwhile, had little say in the matter. Most of them had granted the international companies concessions to produce oil and made their money from royalties and taxes on crude that belonged to the concessionaires.

Things began to change after World War II. Economic growth pushed up oil demand, and foreign oil was abundant, available from a number of sources besides the Middle East, and cheap. By 1949, the United States had become a net oil importer.

Combined with Cold War security concerns, this important new economic status generated great political worry. But the atmosphere was complicated by antitrust suspicions directed toward the oil companies as the As-Is Agreement, fashioned two decades earlier at Achnacarry, came to light. The government at first encouraged imports because of postwar shortages of heating oil and other products. Eventually, it began to worry about the competitive damage that low-cost imports were inflicting on domestic producers and about the effect that damage had on national security.

Policy sought a balance between the supply and price advantages of imported oil and protection of domestic producers. It was a difficult quest. The initial effort relied on voluntary import restraint by oil companies. When that failed—as diversity of commercial interest promised that it would—the federal government in March 1959 adopted the Mandatory Oil Import Program.

This was as crucial a step as the Texas Railroad Commission's prewar move to market demand prorationing. In general, the program limited U.S. oil imports to 12% of U.S. production during the 11 years that it applied. Its express purpose was to protect the U.S. producing industry in the interest of national security. In particular, the program was a regulatory beast. Diversity of interest generated pressures for exemptions for inland refineries, small refineries, and Western Hemisphere exporters, to name but a few. The program was in nearly constant regulatory flux.

Questionable though its efficiency was, the mandatory import program apportioned surplus production capacity and kept supply in line with demand in the United States and elsewhere until 1970. The regulations remained in place until the Arab embargo of 1973–74 but had little effect in its final years. By 1970, thanks to a long exploration slump and steadily rising demand, production capacity surplus in the United States had essentially ceased to exist. Meanwhile, a then-obscure OPEC was turning 10 years old.

THE
TRANSFER
OF
INFLUENCE

O PEC began with a meeting of Arab producers in Baghdad in September 1960. A price cut by oil companies the month before had angered the producing country governments. Furthermore, Iraq wanted to shut out Egypt, a minor oil producer that had tried to make the Arab League, which it controlled, the center of oil market power.

In addition to Iraq, three Arab producing nations—Saudi Arabia, Kuwait, and Qatar—attended the meeting in Baghdad along with two non-Arab nations, Venezuela (South American) and Iran (Persian). They agreed to form an organization that would coordinate the policies of its members and attempt, among other things, to see that oil companies kept prices stable and at least coordinated with them before making changes. The founding OPEC members did not seek to form a cartel and, in fact, could not; at that time, they did not produce any oil of their own.

Although it attended the Baghdad meeting, Qatar did not join the organization until 1961. Eventually, there would be 13 members. Libya and Indonesia joined in 1962. Abu Dhabi joined in 1967; its membership became that of the United Arab Emirates when the federation formed in the 1970s. Algeria joined OPEC in 1969, Nigeria in 1971, Ecuador in 1973, and Gabon in 1975.

In the early years, OPEC's activities focused on establishing a headquarters for its secretariat in Vienna, on coordinating members' policies, and on negotiating with oil companies to improve financial arrangements. Relations between the companies and OPEC members began seriously to change in 1970, when a revolutionary government in Libya successfully demanded lower production and higher prices. The changes touched off a series of comparable actions by other OPEC members and necessitated several important agreements aimed at unifying relationships between members and companies. At this point, the focus of OPEC activity remained on improving members' stances vis-a-vis the oil companies, not on coordinating group production to influence price. U.S. oil import controls and state prorationing systems still balanced supply with demand, although, as noted earlier, depletion of U.S. reserves by 1970 meant that the country essentially was producing at capacity and lacked the market discretion that came with surplus.

THE
ARAB
EMBARGO

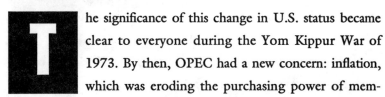

he significance of this change in U.S. status became clear to everyone during the Yom Kippur War of 1973. By then, OPEC had a new concern: inflation, which was eroding the purchasing power of members' dollar-denominated oil revenues. As war broke out on October 6, with Syria and Egypt seeking to reclaim territory occupied by Israel since 1967, OPEC was seeking price increases sufficient to offset past and future deterioration in the dollar's purchasing power. The group also demanded a way to keep posted prices, on which its members' oil earnings were based, permanently above realized (market) prices. Uncertainties of war in an already tight market naturally raised market prices, enabling Persian Gulf members of OPEC to raise posted prices from $3 to $5.12/bbl. This 70% price hike followed unsuccessful negotiations between members and oil companies. Meanwhile, Iraq nationalized Exxon and Mobil interests in Basrah Petroleum Company and called on other Arab states to follow suit.[3]

On October 17, oil ministers of Saudi Arabia, Kuwait, Iraq, Libya, Algeria, Egypt, Abu Dhabi, Bahrain, and Qatar announced a group production cut of 5% and plans for further such cuts in each following month until Israel withdrew from the disputed territories. These countries belonged to a group called the Organization of Arab Petroleum Exporting Countries (OAPEC), to which Syria also belonged. Through the rest of October and into November, OAPEC members began individually to embargo oil shipments to the United States and The Netherlands. By December, Dutch oil supplies had fallen by 30%, prompting the government to declare Israel's occupation of Arab land illegal. Iraq did not support the embargo because it believed that oil company nationalizations were a better way to punish the United States and Holland for their support of Israel.

The embargo lasted until March 19, 1974. During its course, participating exporters met under several auspices—of which OPEC was but one—to try to fashion agreements on oil prices. It was a sloppy process. In January, OPEC managed to boost the posted price once more to $11.65/bbl. By the end of the embargo, however, price strategy disagreements among key exporters were acute, and some of the most aggressive price "hawks" were finding the market resistant to their most extreme price initiatives.

It is important to remember that the embargo was political in nature; it was an attempt by Arab oil exporters, not all of OPEC, to retaliate for American and Dutch support of Israel in the war. But this decidedly political act brought to the forefront economic forces that would reshape the oil market by reshaping relationships among its key players. For one thing, it demonstrated to the world that the United States had lost its petroleum market influence because it no longer controlled sufficient production capacity to maintain a surplus. That influence had transferred to the low-cost, high-capacity producers of the Middle East as well as those other exporters chosen to join the club. Although OAPEC had initiated the embargo and various other Arab groups had exerted pressure during the course of the standoff, it was OPEC, taking in the producing power not just of the Arab exporters but of Iran, Venezuela, Indonesia, and the non-Arab African members as well, that survived as the main arbiter of petroleum supply. It was OPEC, then, that would have to determine who would not produce during periods of market normalcy; that is, during periods when the world did not need as much oil as it could produce.

The embargo had two other important effects. It reoriented the relationships between many important producing countries— including such powerhouses as Kuwait, Saudi Arabia, Abu Dhabi, Venezuela, and Iran—and the oil companies. During the 1970s, all the Arab gulf producers followed the leads of Iraq and Libya with varying degrees of nationalization of oil company interests. Some had negotiated schemes for sharing oil production with the companies; after nationalization, the OPEC states owned all or most of the oil outright.

The embargo's other important effect was its polarization of the world between exporters and importers. OPEC—again, by representing so much of the world's oil production capacity—wielded the power to influence oil prices and had demonstrated that it would exercise that power for political reasons. The industrialized oil consuming world responded by creating the International Energy Agency (IEA) within the Organization for Economic Cooperation and Development. IEA's 23 member countries agreed to maintain individual strategic stockpiles of oil and to share oil in the event of a supply emergency, loosely defined as a 7% shortfall by any member.

The embargo and subsequent shift of oil ownership from companies to producing state governments began a new era of petroleum. It was to be an era with oil companies and U.S. state and federal governments no longer able to influence price, with OPEC members increasingly owning their production capacity and OPEC itself in charge of the world's marginal oil supply, and with the consuming world cast in political opposition to the producers' group.

AFTER THE EMBARGO

or OPEC, history since the embargo has been a long and difficult lesson in petroleum economics, politics, and group dynamics.

The economic lessons began quickly. The price

increases and political backlashes from the embargo ended a long series of strong annual export gains. Between 1968 and 1973, OPEC exports increased at an average rate of 14%/year, reaching 27.55 million B/D in the year the embargo began. The gains ended there. During 1974–79, OPEC exports on an annual basis never returned to the 1973 level, averaging 26.55 million bbl for the six-year period.[4]

Then came the Iranian Revolution of 1978 and 1979. Crude prices shot to $40/bbl on the spot market as Iranian production fell to 2.3 million B/D from as much as 6 million B/D before the oilfield workers strike that preceded revolution. OPEC essentially followed the spot market with a series of increases in member ceiling prices for what had become its benchmark crude—34° gravity Arabian Light. But the ceilings were irrelevant. Members charged what buyers would pay. The marker reached $36/bbl in 1980, with members disagreeing over quality and transportation differentials between the marker and other crudes and generally ignoring organizational agreements.

The heyday did not last. Price rises since the embargo had brought forth production in important areas such as the North Sea and Mexico and cleared away political hurdles to development of supergiant Prudhoe Bay field on Alaska's North Slope. By 1979, the U.S. government had awakened to the folly of oil price controls, which meant that the U.S. market no longer was shielded from the economic compulsions to improve energy consumption efficiency. Requirements for crude oil reached period peaks in the United States of 18.26 million B/D in 1978 and worldwide of 64.5 million B/D in 1979. World requirements for crude fell for four years and did not reattain the 1979 level until 1989. U.S.

requirements for crude have never returned to the 1978 peak level.

OPEC thus faced growing competition from new sources of crude in a shrinking market. Total group exports fell to 22.86 million B/D in 1980 and dropped in each subsequent year to a low of 10.93 million B/D in 1985. It was a market adjusting as markets will to sudden increases in price, and OPEC became its biggest victim.

The group officially faced up to the harsh economic realities of the period in March 1983, when, for the first time in its history, it tried truly to function as a cartel. It dropped the official marker price to $29/bbl from $34 and assigned individual production quotas to its members. This was a stark attempt to prop up the crude price by limiting production and apportioning the pain of deliberately idle production capacity among its members.

It did not work. The failure—and OPEC's inevitable inability to circumvent economic forces—became manifest in 1985, when Saudi Arabia could no longer afford to function as the group's "swing producer." Because of quota cheating by other members, the kingdom was handling the swing producer's job nearly alone. By 1985, market crude prices were $2–$3 barrel below the OPEC marker, and OPEC members were discounting from official prices in order to make sales. In the same year, Saudi production averaged only 3.3 million B/D—a rate so low that associated gas production threatened to become insufficient for the country's domestic needs. Facing gas shortages and plummeting oil revenues, Saudi Arabia knocked supports totally away from the crude price by raising its production and selling at deep discounts, grabbing market share from other OPEC members and forcing many high-cost producers elsewhere in the world out of business.

OPEC'S
PROBLEMS

t no point in OPEC's history can it be said that the group successfully set the price of oil and held it at some target level for any appreciable period. To the contrary, OPEC has nearly always reacted to market forces rather than dictated them to its advantage. It has been able to create temporary distortions, just as the United States was able to artificially limit crude oil and product prices for a few years in the 1970s. Like all such manipulations, however, OPEC's efforts ultimately have succumbed to the pressures of supply and demand.

Cartels usually fail, and OPEC has not always tried to operate as one. Successful cartel action requires a convergence of interest among members that does not exist within OPEC and never will. To support prices, a cartel must be able to enforce production restraint among its members. This requires a discipline OPEC has never been able to muster. Even during 1983–85, when OPEC was supposedly levitating oil prices with production restraint, it was Saudi Arabia that exercised most of the forebearance, while other members yielded to temptations to overproduce. Loss of Saudi patience—or, more accurately, the end of its ability to make sacrifices for the benefit of others—was inevitable.

Diversity of interest made for rocky enforcement of the Achnacarry Agreement in the Middle East before OPEC, led to cheating and freeloading on the prorationing schemes of U.S. states, and kept the Mandatory Oil Import Program in a perpetual state of regulatory change. It also keeps OPEC from acting in unison on oil production and price. Tables 7–1 and 7–3 show why

TABLE 7-3
OPEC'S DISTRIBUTION OF WEALTH

ta	Population, 1989 (1,000)	GNP, 1989 (Million dollars)	GNP per capita, 1989 (Dollars)	Reserves per capita (Barrels)
Iraq	17,757	66,000	3,717	5,630
Iran	50,204	154,585	3,190	1,850
Kuwait	2,020	32,295	16,380	46,530
Saudi Arabia	14,435	85,957	6,020	17,860
Venezuela	19,244	41,462	2,450	3,070
Qatar	330	5,889	17,846	11,210
Libya	4,395	*23,514	*5,410	5,190
Indonesia	178,000	89,371	500	40
U.A.E.	1,550	27,387	17,669	63,290
Algeria	24,453	45,919	2,220	380
Nigeria	113,665	27,533	250	160
Ecuador	10,329	9,668	1,020	150
Gabon	1,105	3,119	2,960	630

*1988 data.

Source: *International Statistics Sourcebook*, PennWell Books, for population, GNP, and per capita GNP data; author's calculations based on reserves from Table 7-1 for per capita reserves.

this always will be so.

There is a fundamental divergence of interest between countries with high reserves lives and low populations and those with low reserves lives and high populations. The former countries, mainly the Arab producers along the Persian Gulf, have come to favor price moderation. They want to assure future generations of markets for oil, which they know their reserves will yield in abundance for many decades. By contrast, the high-population countries usually face strong political pressure to generate revenues as quickly as possible. The pressure becomes acute in such countries that also are relatively poor; that is, the countries with low per-capita gross national product. With comparatively low reserves-to-production ratios, these countries know their production levels must decline fairly soon. They therefore tend to want to make as much money on existing production as possible and often push for the highest possible price, whatever the effect on future demand.

The price moderates usually manage to keep the hawks in line. Indeed, the circumstances of reserves and production capacity that incline them toward price moderation give them the power to enforce their wishes by overproducing whenever they think prices have climbed too much. So what, regarding oil prices, is "too much"? For the power producers in OPEC, it is the price at which demand begins to suffer and alternative fuels become attractive. Especially since 1986, OPEC's most far-sighted producers have become increasingly sophisticated market watchers and have accepted their role of adjusting supply to accommodate near term fluctuations in demand. They also have become diplomats of mixed success, able to find ways to satisfy the revenue urgencies of politically distressed members and still keep production within economic bounds—or at least seem to do so.

The common view is that the price crash engineered by Saudi Arabia in 1985 and 1986 signified the beginning of the end for OPEC. It is probably more accurate to say that the experience taught key members of OPEC and the world that the group's influence has limits; that consumers have influence, too; and that reasonable alignment of production with some level of demand consistent with general economic growth is the best strategy for producers and consumers alike.

AN ADMINISTERED PRICE?

To some outsiders, this behavior of OPEC, this deliberate apportioning of the spare production capacity that usually exists, amounts to a price support system. An OPEC decision to maintain some measure of idle production capacity to some degree allows a comparable measure of more costly capacity to operate elsewhere. Economic theory considers this untenable. It allows price to exceed the marginal production cost, which produces unsustainable economic rents.

While the argument makes economic sense, its usefulness is questionable. The problem is determining marginal production costs in the real world. To be sure, economists can estimate technical production costs with fair accuracy. And these certainly cover a wide spectrum, with the Persian Gulf OPEC producers on the low end, U.S. stripper well operators on the high end, and the North Sea, Mexico, and Venezuela somewhere in the middle. And it is, indeed, true that when Kuwait and Saudi Arabia are producing at 70% of capacity and everyone else is at full flow, the technically cheapest production is yielding to something costlier. The result is price above the theoretical marginal cost of production. Idle cheap capacity enables the marginal cost to be determined by capacity that would not be economic otherwise.

In fact, however, a compelling case can be made that true production costs in places such as Saudi Arabia and Kuwait are significantly higher than technical costs. When a company estimates technical costs it includes some complement of overhead expenses—such as salaries and administrative costs. In Saudi Arabia and Kuwait, overheads include the costs of operating entire countries. The low production costs so often attributed to Persian Gulf producers never reflect these overheads. If they did, the resulting marginal costs would not fall so far below market commodity prices, and economic rents would not look so excessive.[5]

Furthermore, the necessity for a match between price and marginal costs of production applies more easily to manufacturing than it does to production of strategic commodities. Indeed, the measurement of marginal production costs leaves much room for error, given the wide variety of producing environments, different distances from markets, and—as indicated above—special cost considerations for state owned companies in economies centered on petroleum. To say price must equal marginal production cost is to leave great leeway in the determination of price.

Besides, the market does not work that way. When OPEC ministers meet to determine production policies and target prices, they do not focus on marginal production costs. They talk about revenue needs, comparative production capacities, and—in their best moments—how much oil the market requires from them. To repeat, OPEC ministers ultimately act in accordance with what they perceive to be the best interests of their countries. And the countries represented in OPEC have very divergent interests.

What the market wants from OPEC is enough oil to satisfy

demand not fulfilled by all other producers in the world, with enough production capacity kept idle but ready to meet expected demand growth plus unexpected increases. The extent to which the crude price may exceed the marginal cost of production can usefully be viewed as the premium the market must pay for this safety cushion.

OPEC bears the burden of holding idle production capacity during periods of market normalcy (surplus). OPEC, therefore, collects the premium, after consumption taxes—or as much of a premium as the market allows. The market demands a surplus, yet oil—because the market is a closed system—cannot be produced at will. There always must be an entity able and willing to withhold production. The market always must pay for the service. In the modern petroleum age, the job and whatever challenges and rewards go with it belong to OPEC.

REFERENCES

1. Vietor, Richard H.K., *Energy Policy in America Since 1945: A Study in Business-Government Relations,* Cambridge University Press, Cambridge, 1984. Much of the material on U.S. prorationing and the Mandatory Oil Import Program comes from this source.

2. Ghanem, Shakri M., *OPEC: The Rise and Fall of an Exclusive Club,* KPI Limited, London, 1986. Much of the material on OPEC history comes from this source.

3. *Chronology of the Arab Oil Embargo,* American Petroleum Institute, 1983.

4. Data on OPEC exports and world requirements for crude come from *Energy Statistics Sourcebook,* PennWell Books, 1991.

5. Robinson, Silvan, " 'Real' Cost Base of Oil Isn't What You Think," *Petroleum Intelligence Weekly,* April 3, 1989.

CHAPTER EIGHT

TAKING
STOCK
OF
INVENTORIES

Petroleum does not travel through the closed system we know as the market at a steady speed. Consumers do not use petroleum products at precisely the same rate at which refineries make them. Refineries do not process crude oil at precisely the same rate that the crude arrives by way of pipelines, tank trucks, and barges. And the transportation system does not carry crude at precisely the same rate at which the substance is produced in the field. In time, of course, these rates balance one another; supply must equal demand in the end because it is a closed system. But something must balance the intermittent discrepancies between production, processing, transportation, and consumption rates. And that something is storage capacity, in which reside inventories, also known as

Storage often begins where oil is produced, on the lease. These tanks sit on a lease in East Texas.

stocks.

Inventories provide an important swing factor between supply and demand. When production falls short of demand, withdrawals from inventory make up the difference. When production exceeds demand, oil flows into storage, and there is an inventory build. Of course, stock withdrawals and builds, like everything else in the oil market, have their limits. For withdrawals, the limit is the amount of accessible oil remaining in inventory. For stock builds, the limit is available storage capacity. As long as there is room for stock levels to fluctuate, however, inventories cannot be ignored in the question of how much oil the world can, or will, deliver to market. They play a role in the answer that is by no means passive; owners of storage capacity and stored oil can and do exert considerable discretion in stock levels. The discretion is partly strategic, partly operational, and partly commercial. And the cumulative effects of decisions reflecting that discretion—stock levels and trends for crude and individual products—exert strong, often dominant, influence in crude and product prices.

TYPES
OF
INVENTORIES

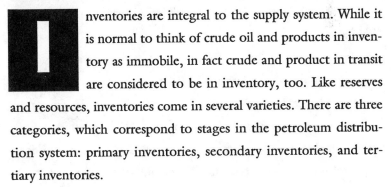

nventories are integral to the supply system. While it is normal to think of crude oil and products in inventory as immobile, in fact crude and product in transit are considered to be in inventory, too. Like reserves and resources, inventories come in several varieties. There are three categories, which correspond to stages in the petroleum distribution system: primary inventories, secondary inventories, and tertiary inventories.

The physical distinctions among these categories are important. Even more important to the analyst, however, are the relative abilities with which stocks in each category can be measured. Simply put, the information system keeps track of primary inventories with a fair degree of accuracy. The ability to measure stocks begins to break down as products move into the secondary and tertiary stages of the system, where inventories certainly exist but are much more variable and disperse. According to one estimate, reporting systems cover 75% of all primary inventories; namely, those in Europe, Japan, and the United States. Primary inventories in smaller industrialized countries and in the developing world must be estimated based upon what is known about petroleum operations there. The size of secondary and tertiary inventories is not known; together, they may exceed primary stocks.[1]

Inventory measurements, therefore, nearly always concentrate on primary stocks. This raises a point crucial to petroleum economic analysis: Most reports of petroleum demand measure deliveries from primary storage, not actual consumption. Reporting mechanisms can keep fairly accurate account of the former but not of the latter. It is much easier to count gallons of gasoline departing five refineries in a region, for example, than it is to measure gasoline actually burned in the five million vehicles that may travel within and through the area.

It is possible, therefore, for measured demand to differ significantly from actual consumption. When secondary and tertiary stocks build, demand measured on the basis of deliveries from primary storage overstates actual consumption. When secondary and tertiary stocks decrease, demand measured the usual way understates volumes actually consumed. Secondary and tertiary stock builds must always follow drawdowns, however; the fluctuations balance over time. Over time, therefore, deliveries from primary storage most accurately depict demand trends: first, because they are most readily measured and second, because they smooth out the downstream stock fluctuations that elude reporting systems.

So what equipment holds stocks in these categories? Generally, it is anything that performs the market's essential function of containing petroleum. It may be useful to refer back to the diagram of the distribution system in Chapter 3.

Primary stocks include oil in gathering systems and lease tanks in producing areas. In crude oil storage terminals and transportation networks, primary stocks include volumes in pipelines, tankers, barges, tanks, railroad tank cars, and tank trucks. At refineries, primary stocks include crude, unfinished oil, and finished products in tanks as well as oil in process units and equipment. And in the product transportation network, primary stocks include oil in pipelines, tankers, barges, tanks, tank cars, and tank trucks. Primary inventories also include government-owned stocks, such as the Strategic Petroleum Reserve in the United States.

Secondary stocks include oil at bulk plants, fuel oil dealers, and gasoline and diesel retail outlets.

Tertiary stocks include products in the hands of consumers: gasoline in automobile and tractor tanks, fuel oil in factories, jet fuel in airport and military base storage and in fuel tanks of aircraft, heating oil in commercial establishments and homes, and any other oil in the possession of its final user.[2]

Most storage capacity takes the form of fixed, onshore facilities such as tanks and pipelines. Maximum capacity, therefore, would seem to have definite limits. To increase holding capacity, refiners or terminal operators would have to build new tanks, which might require costly land purchases as well as substantial construction costs. In fact, storage capacity's upper limit is more flexible than that. Tanker slow-steaming, for example, can increase the amount of inventory on the water at certain times. And when enough hulls are available, tankers can be pressed into service for storage, laden and moored near markets thought to require a supply buffer.

OPEC exporters have used tankers in this way during periods of overproduction and when crises, such as the Iraq-Kuwait war, threatened. It can be costly, especially when the tanker market is healthy and the hulls used for storage could be employed more profitably in the shipping trade (Table 8–1). When no crisis looms, an increase in floating storage signals production competition within OPEC. The costly addition to storage capacity then represents an expensive, temporary holding tactic for volumes produced but not sold. The costs of holding such volumes generate growing incentives to sell the stored crude at whatever price is required to move it into the market—which ultimately weakens prices. In fact, excessive inventory growth usually induces traders to dampen bid prices even before the stored crude becomes available for sale.

How Much Can Be Used?

n the commercial (non–government-owned) primary distribution system, a certain amount of oil considered to be held in inventory is not really available for consumption. This has to do with the physical reali-

TABLE 8–1
TANKERS USED TO STORE OIL

	1978	1979	1980	1981	1982	1983	1984	1985	1986	1987	1988	1989	1990	1991
						(Million metric tons deadweight at midyear)								
Oil company owned	0.83	0.75	1.91	3.20	5.61	4.45	7.25	6.18	7.51	5.71	4.22	3.43	4.86	5.88
Independently owned	2.15	6.03	8.99	16.21	12.64	10.50	13.39	12.64	10.55	11.06	7.50	6.09	8.63	15.02
Total*	2.98	6.78	10.91	19.41	18.24	14.95	20.64	18.82	18.06	16.77	11.72	9.51	13.48	20.90
Location:														
Middle East	0.23	0.47	0.84	0.76	0.48	0.51	3.04	3.90	6.81	7.73	6.25	4.07	5.77	7.02
Far East	0.78	5.73	6.96	11.95	11.34	10.05	12.97	9.17	6.60	4.16	2.67	2.57	2.43	4.83
U.S. Gulf/Caribbean	1.89	0.27	2.26	4.59	5.06	2.45	1.26	1.76	1.26	0.58	0.52	0.67	2.40	1.80
Other areas	0.08	0.31	0.84	2.10	1.36	1.94	3.37	3.99	3.40	4.30	2.29	2.21	2.88	7.25

*Elements may not add to totals due to rounding.

Source: Cambridge Energy Research Associates *World Oil Trends*, from Lloyds Shipping List data.

ties of distribution equipment and operation.

One of the best descriptions of the commercial primary storage system comes from the National Petroleum Council, a group of oil industry experts that conducts studies at the request of the U.S. Secretary of Energy. Although the description, part of a study the department asks NPC to conduct from time to time, applies to the U.S. storage system, other countries have comparable systems, and the same principles apply.

NPC identifies seven basic components of primary inventory and storage capacity: (1) unavailable inventory and (2) working inventory, which together make up (3) minimum operating inventory; (4) operating space, which added to minimum operating inventory yields (5) maximum operating inventory; and (6) contingency space and (7) unavailable space, which added to maximum operating inventory yields the total capacity of the system (see Figure 8–1).

Unavailable inventory is the crude or product in pipelines and other transportation containers, refinery equipment, and tank bottoms that cannot be removed without shutting down whatever contains it. Pipelines, for example, must be full of oil in order to operate. When oil is forced into the upstream end of a full pipeline, an equivalent amount of oil flows out of the other end, which is how pipelines are supposed to work. But the volume needed to keep the pipeline full—called pipeline fill—is not available for consumption. Similarly, oil in transit by barge, tanker, truck, or rail car is unavailable while in transit. The normal volume of oil in transit is thus considered unavailable inventory, although specific cargoes certainly do reach market eventually.

The same thing happens in refinery processing units: They

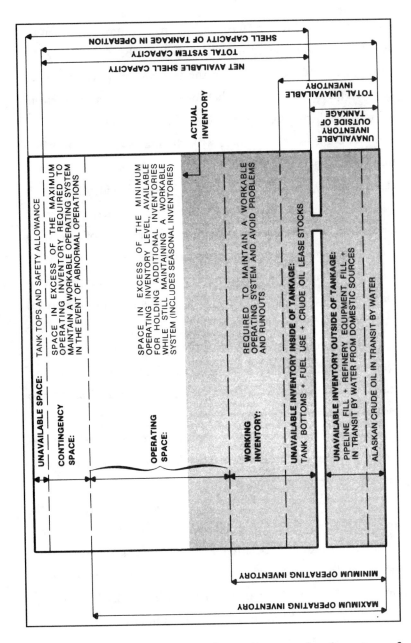

Fig. 8–1. Categories of petroleum inventories (courtesy of National Petroleum Council).

always must contain some feedstock or product in volumes unavailable to the market. And most tanks cannot be drained dry. By design, a layer of oil remains in the bottoms of tanks considered empty. This keeps impurities that settle to the bottom from escaping into the distribution system downstream of storage.

Working inventories deal with the practicalities of distribution system operation. A refinery, for example, processes crude oil at fairly steady rates. Crude deliveries by tanker and product offtake by tank truck obviously do not occur at such even rates. Crude and product inventories solve this problem of operating cycles. They also provide a buffer against system interruptions, such as late crude deliveries, pipeline shutdowns, and refinery closures. Working inventories also hold unfinished products in preparation for blending.

Minimum operating inventories vary from company to company and from refinery to refinery. They depend on demand and crude supply patterns, transportation types and capacities, and the availability of alternative supplies, processing, and transportation strategies. A refiner usually does not draw below the level of minimum operating inventory because to do so would in one way or another compromise operations.

Operating space is the discretional portion of stocks. It is storage space available for inventories above minimum operating levels. Companies use operating space to handle seasonal demand swings, building stocks of specific products in their low-demand times of year (gasoline in winter, for example, and distillate heating oil in summer). Refiners also build stocks in advance of planned shutdowns for maintenance.

Maximum operating inventories are levels above which the

system cannot operate normally. The capacity above maximum operating levels includes unavailable space—tank tops and safety allowance—and contingency space, essentially a safety cushion against disruptions, such as shutdown of a downstream products pipeline.

GOVERNMENT STOCKS

In response to the Arab oil embargo of 1973–74, most industrialized countries adopted schemes for stockpiling oil against emergency supply interruptions. The International Energy Agency, for example, requires its 23 members to hold or mandate the private holding of stocks sufficient to meet net import requirements at current levels for 90 days. This strategic stockpiling supports an oil-sharing system that IEA members have agreed to implement whenever any member experiences a 7% emergency shortage.

The United States, Germany, Japan, and Sweden opted for government-owned strategic inventories. In the United States, the system is called the Strategic Petroleum Reserve, under which the government buys crude for storage in salt dome caverns in Texas and Louisiana. The SPR eventually is to hold 1 billion bbl of crude oil.

Elsewhere, except for New Zealand and Canada, governments do not own stocks but rather require companies to reserve specified volumes of oil in inventory for strategic use. New Zealand and Canada have no strategic inventory programs. Except for the United States, the countries with government-owned stocks mandate industry strategic reserves as well.

Strategic inventories have not been directly used on any significant scale since their inceptions in the mid-1970s. The United States implemented a modest drawdown from its SPR during the 1990–91 crisis in Iraq and Kuwait. The existence of a large strategic-buffer supply has indirect consequences, nevertheless. It certainly discourages politically motivated export embargoes by reducing chances that supply mischief can have immediate effects. And it to some extent has reduced the volume of oil private companies feel obliged to hold in inventory beyond mandated and operationally necessary levels.

How
Much
Inventory?

The main analytical question regarding inventories is sufficiency in relation to demand. Are stock volumes high enough to keep oil flowing smoothly to consumers at anticipated levels of consumption? The question has two main variables: demand and what inventory managers, including governments, consider sufficient coverage.

Demand is the easier of the two variables to analyze. Obviously, the world needs greater oil stocks with demand at 60 million B/D than it would with demand 10% or 15% lower. To account for varying levels of demand, inventory planners relate inventory levels to current levels of consumption in a measurement called days' supply. The arithmetic is simple: To arrive at days' supply, divide primary inventories by current daily consumption. To arrive at inventory volumes needed to attain some target days' supply level, multiply current daily consumption by the target number of days.

For strategic inventories, governments have simply asserted target days' supply levels. As indicated earlier, the IEA employs a variation based on import levels, requiring members to maintain 90 days' coverage. The European Community, by contrast, bases its compulsory petroleum stock levels on current consumption.

Petroleum economic analysis uses days' supply based on primary stocks and current consumption to assess adequacy of inventory coverage. There are technical problems with doing so, the main one being that not all oil in primary storage is available for consumption. It can safely be assumed, however, that secondary and tertiary stocks offset the unavailable portion of primary inventories. On the regional or global scope with which economic analysis is concerned, days' supply provides an adequate basis for historic comparison. If inventories have represented an average of 90 days of consumption in the first quarter of each of the past five years in the industrialized world and there have been no problems, and if they represent 85 days' consumption in the first quarter this year, what is the reason? Is there a potential supply problem? Those are the types of questions that the analyst asks with regard to inventories over large regions or worldwide. Table 8–2 tracks onshore stocks in the industrialized world on a quarterly basis.

Companies use refinements of days' supply analysis to help them determine how much oil to hold in storage. But many other factors come into play. A refiner, for example, knows its minimum inventory level and maximum holding capacity. It knows its operating cycles and how much discretionary inventory it must hold in

TABLE 8-2
STOCKS ON LAND IN OECD COUNTRIES

Closing stocks	Total*	——Volume—— Government controlled (Million metric tons)	Companies	Total*	——Consumption coverage—— Government controlled (Days of forward consumption**)	Companies
1984						
First quarter	439	105	334	95	23	72
1985						
First quarter	414	106	309	99	25	74
Second quarter	421	108	313	98	25	73
Third quarter	419	115	303	93	26	67
Fourth quarter	429	118	311	93	25	67
1986						
First quarter	416	113	303	94	25	69
Second quarter	428	114	315	96	25	71
Third quarter	454	115	338	98	25	73
Fourth quarter	444	118	328	94	25	69
1987						
First quarter	429	119	310	97	27	70
Second quarter	432	120	312	95	26	68
Third quarter	453	122	331	96	26	70
Fourth quarter	457	126	331	95	26	69
1988						
First quarter	440	129	311	98	29	69
Second quarter	454	129	325	98	28	70
Third quarter	462	129	332	92	26	66
Fourth quarter	451	132	319	92	27	65
1989						
First quarter	445	134	311	97	29	68
Second quarter	453	134	319	97	29	68
Third quarter	466	138	331	93	27	66
Fourth quarter	456	136	319	93	28	65
1990						
First quarter	466	138	328	100	30	70
Second quarter	477	139	338	98	29	70
Third quarter	478	139	339	100	29	71
Fourth quarter	470	138	331	97	28	68
1991						
First quarter	461	136	324	99	29	69
Second quarter	464	136	327	99	29	70
Third quarter	477	137	340	97	28	69
Fourth quarter	466	139	328	94	28	66
1992						
First quarter	454	141	313	97	30	67
Second quarter	459	141	318	96	29	67
Third quarter	466	141	325	94	28	66

Note: OECD is Organization for Economic Cooperation and Development.
Members are Canada, United States, Australia, Japan, New Zealand, Austria,
Belgium, Denmark, Finland, France, Germany, Greece, Ireland, Italy, Luxembourg,
Netherlands, Norway, Portugal, Spain, Sweden, Switzerland, Turkey, and United
Kingdom.
*May not add due to rounding. **Based on actual sales except 1992, which uses
latest forecast.
Source: International Energy Agency *Monthly Oil Market Report.*

order to keep things running smoothly. It also knows the extent to which seasonal demand changes affect its business and what maintenance shutdowns it plans. These factors vary enough from refiner to refiner to make generalities about desired inventory levels difficult.

It is useful, however, to know some of the factors that influence inventory decisions. At one time, refiners used inventories of their two main products, gasoline and distillate heating oil, to balance seasonal demand swings. Unable to exercise much discretion in product yields, they operated capacity at utilization levels needed to meet gasoline demand during the Northern Hemisphere's peak consumption months of summer and stored the distillate they could not keep from producing for the winter, when it would be in demand. In the winter, the storage cycle reversed. In terms of operating strategy, this worked fairly well, although inventory imbalances occurred in those years when a winter of low distillate demand followed a summer of high gasoline use.

More recently, at least in the industrialized world, refiners have installed conversion capacities that give them increasing control over product yields. In summer, they can meet gasoline demand without producing as much immediately unnecessary distillate as before. With wintertime changes in processing they can meet distillate demand without overproducing gasoline relative to requirements. As a result, they need less product inventories on average and less storage capacity overall.

This reduced need for inventories creates significant economic benefits. As in any business, inventories in the oil industry represent costs. Fixed investments in tanks require capital. And inventories require working capital, the costs of which track short-term interest rates. Money tied up in stored oil—that is, oil not turning immediately into sales revenues—is money that cannot be used for other investments. When interest rates rise, the costs of holding inventory (carrying costs) rise proportionately.

In the early 1980s, shrinking oil demand reduced the operational needs for refiners to hold inventories. And sharp rises in interest rates gave them the financial incentive not just to reduce stocks but also to find ways to reduce inventory needs in relation to a given demand level. This pressure to keep inventories at minimum levels influenced refiners' decisions during the period to invest in the conversion capacity that improved flexibility of product yields. At the same time, growth in compulsory or government-owned stocks eased the pressure on refiners to hold stocks against unexpected supply interruptions.

Even with the increased conversion capacity in place, interest rates remain crucial to inventory decisions. Refiners tend to carry less inventory when interest rates are high than when they are low. The reason is simple, rising interest rates raise inventory carrying costs. Supply strategy considerations remain strong, however. Few refiners will gamble against shortage for the sake of interest charge savings that all of them recognize as a regular cost of conducting business.

MANAGING INVENTORIES FOR PROFIT

odern processing flexibility gives refiners another potential use of stocks: Effective inventory management can be profitable. Less locked into seasonal inventory cycles than they were before, refiners can use inventories to seek trading profits.

Most oil companies have approached trading activities with great caution. Well they should. They exist to earn profits by selling oil products from the crude oil that they produce (or purchase) and process. Those physical activities require maintenance of inventories at some level. It would be imprudent for a company to compromise its operations with a commitment for delivery from essential working inventories under some third-party trading deal. As long as a company preserves its working inventories, however, it can be just as imprudent not to take advantage of trading opportunities that arise.

When crude prices are rising, for example, a company can buy now to sell at a higher price later if it has somewhere to store the commodity. Similarly, a refiner convinced that the crude price will rise during the next month can reduce its costs by buying twice the volume of crude it needs this month and storing the excess. Then, when it processes the stored crude in the following month, crude costs are lower than they would have been if it had gone to the market for its crude needs. For this to be profitable, of course, the price increase must more than offset the inventory carrying costs. The motivations work in reverse when the crude price is declining. If a refiner is convinced that next month's crude price will be lower than it is now, it makes no sense to buy for storage.

This, in very simple terms, is how physical trading works. Because of price volatility in the modern petroleum market, most oil companies have established trading operations both to ensure they meet their feedstock needs and to earn profits from the profitable timing of commodity purchases and from third-party deals. The characteristic caution with which most companies approach trading comes from two important realizations. One is the basic trading risk of making the wrong assumption about future price. The other is the disadvantage many companies feel they face (technically and operationally oriented as most are) in competition against financially oriented trading professionals.

Trading considerations may, therefore, influence inventory levels if enough owners of storage capacity all reach essentially the same judgment about future prices and take essentially the same action in response at about the same time. But the extent of such influence is seldom clear. When commercial days' supply departs noticeably from recent trends, the availability of relatively safe trading profits to oil companies and terminal operators may provide the explanation.

THOSE
INVENTORY
PROFITS

Trading profits must be distinguished from inventory profits, which are more of an accounting phenomenon and can be deceiving. Inventory profits result from the effects of price changes on inventory valuations or from a switch from one method of assigning values to inventories to another. There are two main ways of evaluating inventories: the last-in, first-out (LIFO) method and the first-in, first-out (FIFO) method. As the name suggests, LIFO accounting assumes that the most recently acquired inventories are sold first. FIFO assumes first sales of the oldest inventories.

When prices rise, inventory values are greater under FIFO than under LIFO. Because of this discrepancy, cost of goods sold is less under FIFO, which makes gross profit greater, everything else being equal. Under both accounting methods, an inventory draw during a period of rising prices creates profits for the period of accounting—inventory profits. But inventory profits create a problem: An inventory draw now necessitates a buildup later. If prices are still climbing when the buildup occurs, inventory profits turn into losses.

There are two discretionary factors at work here. Within regulatory and professional accounting standard limits, companies can elect their inventory accounting method. And they certainly control their inventory levels. In theory, then, they can influence profits within a specific period solely by how they account for and manage their physical oil stocks. In the United States, most major oil companies prefer LIFO for most or all of their oil inventories. LIFO aligns costs of goods sold more closely to replacement costs than does FIFO. And by tending to understate gross revenues in periods of rising prices, it results in a lower tax burden for profitable companies.

So the prospect of inventory profits may, at times, affect inventory levels. A company might have financial reasons to draw down inventories during a certain period in order to report the associated earnings gain. The problem is that the withdrawn inventory probably will have to be replaced at greater cost, since it was rising prices that made inventory profits possible in the first place. This will offset the current period's profit gain with a later period's cost increase.

On balance, the analyst must recognize that commercial considerations, such as interest rates and the chance for trading and inventory profits, exert strong pressures in decisions concerning commercial inventories. Improvements in refining flexibility have made seasonal inventory balancing less important than it once was. And growth in government and compulsory stocks have eased the requirement of companies to maintain a storage cushion for strategic reasons. Inventories increasingly behave according to complex motivations that may not apply across the market. They thus can be difficult to predict or explain. But they are a pivotal factor in the amount of oil available to the market and thus often function as a strong determinant of price.

REFERENCES

1. *World Oil Inventories,* Exxon Background Series, Exxon Corp., 1981.

2. *Petroleum Storage and Transportation,* Vol. IV, *Petroleum Inventories and Storage,* National Petroleum Council, 1989.

CHAPTER NINE

TRADING
AHEAD

As the preceding chapters have attempted to make clear, the modern oil market has become something quite different from its forebears. Although the law of supply and demand works no more or less vigorously now than ever, the machinations by which the law plays out have drastically changed.

Early in the petroleum industry's history, integrated oil companies managed supply, demand, and price. Their influence derived from the large share of the world's production, manufacturing (processing), and distribution capacity under their collective control. They could not control demand, but they could count on its increasing over time. They could not totally control supply, but they could use their political influence to win U.S. production controls, import limits, and tariffs. With investments in both raw-material production and manufacturing, the integrated majors enjoyed upstream profit gains when crude prices rose and downstream profits when they fell. They favored market stability, and their structures and behaviors promoted the same.

Futures prices influence refiners' decisions about how much crude oil and petroleum products to hold in inventory.

Nationalization of oil company production assets by producing nation governments, the pivotal phenomenon of the 1960s and 1970s, severed integrated companies from much of their raw material. While integrated companies remain in business, integration in the past two decades has not been the market force that it was before. Influence over crude-oil supply is concentrated within a group of exporting nations whose political and economic interests seldom converge.

Meanwhile, the manufacturing segment of the market—

refining—has had to accommodate striking changes in demand patterns. In general, the market has required proportionately more light products, such as gasoline and diesel fuel, and less heavy residual fuels. Because average crude quality has not improved accordingly, refiners have had to invest in increasingly sophisticated internal processing equipment. The aim is to upgrade the heavy products of distillation into the lighter ones demanded by consumers. Decelerating overall demand growth has compounded the financial problems associated with these investments. Unlike the refining industry's first major round of distillation-centered investment, this modern upgrade-centered round has had to be planned and executed under conditions of daunting price uncertainty. Investors cannot expect to know much about future crude costs or do much directly to influence this crucial component of refining economics. And, with so many refiners and retailers at work in the market, no entity comparable to OPEC exists to manage processing capacity excesses that occur in periods of slack demand. The downstream industry, in other words, is more fragmented than its upstream counterpart. And it must contend with price uncertainty in a period when investment needs are great.

Obviously, no single entity has significant influence over both upstream and downstream markets, even though those markets influence each other as much as ever, if not more. The result is what often is called increasing volatility; that is, crude and product prices change more frequently and to a greater degree than they did before. This may not be entirely accurate. In an earlier age, crude prices did not stray much from the $3/bbl level, and long-term contracts were the rule. Now prices seldom drop into single-digit levels, computers provide instant information on transactions, and there are more transactions than there were before due to industry deintegration and the dominant role of spot and short-term trading. Comparing the periods can be misleading. A 30¢ price swing is a 10% change with an oil price of $3/bbl but less than 2% with a starting price of $18. And it is probably true that prices change more now than they did in the noncomputerized era simply because there are more transactions now. But there was no way to know and record the price of every transaction in the earlier era; maybe what was reported simply could not sample the prices that deviated most from the norm. Much of what some see as volatility today is the proliferation of price data that is available now and was not before. Certainly, there are many more types of transactions and more ways to measure price movements now. And information about price movements is more widely available and travels almost instantaneously, which itself influences subsequent deals. It is safe to say that prices are much less predictable now than they were in the simpler age.

This uncertainty has intensified an important dimension of risk in oil industry operations—the risk of being wrong about future price. Less able than they were prior to industry deintegration to manage supply and, to some extent, price, oil companies now must manage risk. They do so to an increasing degree by trading in the forward and futures markets.

These markets evolved naturally and inevitably as the market became more fragmented and less stable. They sometimes are blamed for increasing the market's volatility, and to some extent they must plead guilty to the charge: Program trading (automatic futures-market transactions that traders undertake to defend themselves against surprise price movements) can exaggerate market corrections. In much greater measure, however, futures markets result from, rather than cause, the price instability that has come to characterize the modern oil market. To industry participants they provide essential risk management tools. To speculators they offer opportunities for trading profits. And to industry analysts they afford a continuous, up-to-the-minute gauge of oil-market conditions.

PRICE UNCERTAINTY AND REPLACEMENT SUPPLY

Nothing about the oil industry's recent changes has diminished the importance of replacement supply to all participants in the market. A producer, refiner, or marketer that does not replace what it sells is, by definition, liquidating its inventories (or reserves, in the case of the producer) and its business. Beyond that commercial reality, the oil industry's characteristic operating delays and investment lead times become hazards in conditions of changing prices. Months or years can pass between a discovery and first commercial production, or between the decision to purchase a refinery alkylation unit and first returns on the investment. Weeks pass between the purchase of crude oil at Ras Tanura and delivery in Rotterdam or Houston. More weeks can pass between crude delivery and processing, and between processing and sale of the resulting products. A disadvantageous price change during the course of these normal operating cycles can be ruinous to the crude or product owner.

When near-term price movements were more predictable than they are today—near-term meaning coincident with operating cycles—market participants could manage price risks with inventories. A refiner anticipating a crude-oil price increase could build stocks in advance, to the extent storage space was available. Doing so made economic sense as long as the expected price increase came to pass and its size more than offset carrying charges of the extra crude in storage. What the refiner in effect was doing was building a reservoir of cheap feedstock upon which to draw when the crude price rose. Conversely, a refiner anticipating cheaper crude would benefit by drawing on stocks for feedstock rather than buying crude for immediate processing, making room for cheaper purchases for both processing and storage once the price decline materialized.

To be sure, wrong price predictions could be costly. The refiner who built stocks in preparation for a price rise that never occurred suffered from excessive carrying costs. Worse, if prices fell instead of rose, the refiner liquidating costly crude inventories suffered shrunken or nonexistent margins. Likewise, the refiner drawing stocks before a forecast price drop that turned instead into a gain ended up buying more high-cost feedstock than did competitors who guessed better.

But mistakes did not happen with damaging frequency in the old days. Price changes occurred mainly for seasonal reasons, which made predictions reasonably sound. When mistakes did happen, the costs usually were tolerable. The chance of being wrong about future price movements was an acceptable risk of sound inventory management.

In the age of market fragmentation, there is too much potential for surprise. In the 30 days a volume of crude purchased at $20/bbl might spend in storage at a refinery, product prices can deteriorate to the point that the crude's netback value after processing falls well below the purchase price. It happens. The value of a VLCC cargo of crude purchased fob Ras Tanura can deteriorate in the time it takes the vessel to reach Rotterdam. The refiners who made these purchases have no control over the developments leading to loss. To protect themselves against price jolts, most refiners have resorted to techniques, all based on some form of forward or futures trading, known as hedging.

Hedges take many forms and come in a broad spectrum of complexity. And they are by no means the sole province of refiners: Producers and traders have adopted hedging strategies. Indeed, anyone in the oil market needing to own crude or products for any length of time can use hedging to protect against the risk of price surprise.

A
BASIC
HEDGE

A hedge involves two simultaneous and offsetting transactions, a purchase and a sale with a timing difference between the associated delivery obligations. A forward or futures contract provides the timing difference. Suppose a crude-oil trader plans to buy a cargo of crude oil at Ras Tanura, Saudi Arabia, and to sell it on the spot market in Rotterdam. He obviously believes that he will be able to sell at a price sufficiently in excess of his purchase price to cover the costs of transportation and to earn a profit. But much can happen in the 35–45 days between the time he loads in Ras Tanura and the tanker's arrival in Rotterdam. What if the crude price drops? The problem for the trader is time—that transit period during which events beyond his control might destroy the economics of his deal and sock him with a heavy loss. He can eliminate the risk of that loss if somehow he can take time out of the equation, if he can sell his crude at the price he expects to receive in Rotterdam as soon as he takes delivery in Ras Tanura instead of 35–45 days later. A forward or futures contract enables him to do exactly that.

The trader might know he can buy crude fob at Ras Tanura at $18/bbl and thinks a month later the spot price for Saudi crude in Rotterdam will be $23/bbl. He can charter a tanker at a rate equating to $2/bbl for the voyage, leaving him with a profit of $3/bbl—if the spot market in Rotterdam lives up to his expectations. If spot prices are only $20/bbl when his crude arrives, he only breaks even and has nothing to show for his risks and effort. If spot prices are less than $20, he loses money.

The trader, however, must have had some reason to expect spot prices to be $23/bbl five weeks after he loads in Ras Tanura. Others no doubt harbor similar thoughts. Someone might be willing to risk money on the chance that the spot crude price five weeks hence will be even higher. If so, the trader and the risk-taker, or speculator, can work a forward deal covering the trader's cargo. On the day of loading at Ras Tanura, the trader pays $18/bbl in cash to Saudi Aramco and simultaneously sells an equivalent volume of crude at $23/bbl to the speculator for delivery in Rotterdam on the expected arrival date of the tanker. In other words, he executes a forward sale, locking in the profit margin on which he based the economics of his trade. He has hedged against the risk that the spot crude price in Rotterdam will be less than $23/bbl when his cargo arrives. He also has forgone any chance for additional profits in the event that the spot price exceeds $23. That opportunity now belongs to the speculator who purchased the cargo five weeks forward.

This is a simplistic example of how a forward trade works. But it demonstrates the very different motivations of the two essential parties: the hedger wishing to reduce price risks associated with ownership of a physical commodity and the speculator willing to assume risks in hopes of large profits and usually having no interest in physical ownership. It also demonstrates the crucial consideration of timing, in this case the transit period during which a potential price drop presented the trader with an unacceptable measure of risk. In real life, hedging strategies become much more complicated than this example. Any hedging strategy, however, makes use of some form of contract that introduces a delivery timing discrepancy and thereby provides a means of transferring risk from someone who does not want it to someone who does.

THE
MARKETS

ifferent though they be in structure and operation, forward and futures markets all perform the same basic function: They arbitrate risks by matching hedgers with speculators. Participants in forward and futures markets do not buy and sell physical barrels of crude oil or product but rather contracts calling for future delivery of physical barrels. Money thus changes hands at the time of the transaction; petroleum changes hands later or not at all in some cases.

Because forward and futures transactions involve contracts, the markets for them are often called paper markets to distinguish them from physical, or cash, markets. Volumes in the paper markets are referred to as dry or paper barrels, those in the physical markets, wet barrels.

Forward and futures markets differ mainly in formality, futures markets being the more formal and structured of the two. Futures contracts are very standardized and trade in central locations called exchanges.

Forward contracts trade directly between the parties and can be much more flexible than futures. Forward markets tend to organize around particular crudes and regions and vary in their degree of structure. Some forward markets, such as the 15-day Brent market, have developed standardized contracts. The forward Brent market is, in fact, a hybrid with some characteristics of a cash market. Similarly, much spot trading has come to incorporate features of forward trading. Many cash transactions delay price determination for some period—transit time of a tanker cargo of crude, for example—to build in protection against unexpected price changes. In fact, the term "forward cash market" has become common. Forward markets also have developed around specific products and locations, taking on catchy names such as Boston Bingo (heating oil), Russian Roulette (gas oil), and Manhattan Mogas (motor gasoline).

As the spot market grew in importance along with the loss of market influence of integrated oil companies, international crude prices came to be determined generally in reference to benchmark crudes. In the early 1990s, the most important reference crudes were West Texas Intermediate (WTI), Alaskan North Slope (ANS), Brent Blend, and Dubai Fateh. Each crude existed in sufficient volume and was widely traded enough to provide what traders call "liquidity," meaning transactions in the crude are fairly accessible and continuous. Each crude, too, was "fungible," meaning it could be traded in place of a number of other crudes without requiring major commercial or chemical adjustments. And each crude served as a basic feedstock in at least one major refining center. Forward markets naturally developed for these benchmark crudes. Eventually, other crudes began to trade at fixed differentials to one or more of the reference grades. The differentials accommodated variations in quality and distance to market, so that a change of price in, say, WTI set off series of price changes in other crudes.

This reference system remains a key element of the market. But futures rather than forward or spot quotations increasingly function as the main proxies of crude and product values. It has become the norm for prices in physical market contracts to be based on the futures contract price for a reference crude on a particular date.

The two most important futures markets are the New York Mercantile Exchange (Nymex) and the International Petroleum Exchange (IPE), based in London. Nymex is the larger of the two in terms of trading volume and number of types of contracts (see Tables 9–1 and 9–2). The underlying commodity of the basic Nymex crude contract began as WTI. Due to declining production rates for that crude, Nymex broadened delivery specifications for its futures contract to include other comparable oils in a category

TABLE 9–1
NEW YORK MERCANTILE EXCHANGE RECORDS*

Contract Date introduced	Volume Date of record	Open Interest Date of record
New York Harbor gasoline futures Dec. 3, 1984	48,910 June 30, 1992	133,136 Dec. 20, 1991
Crude oil futures March 30, 1983	184,876 Aug. 7, 1990	389,313 June 11, 1992
Gulf Coast gasoline futures Sept. 18, 1992	435 Sept. 24, 1992	951 Oct. 8, 1992
Heating oil futures Nov. 14, 1978	64,328 Aug. 20, 1991	152,287 Oct 24, 1991
Natural gas futures April 3, 1990	32,705 Sept. 23, 1992	75,928 Oct. 9, 1992
Propane futures Aug. 21, 1987	835 Jan. 22, 1991	3,952 Sept. 27, 1990
Sour crude oil futures Feb. 28, 1992	1,851 Feb. 28, 1992	1,196 March 4, 1992
Crude oil options Nov. 14, 1986	64,887 May 26, 1992	391,078 July 2, 1992
Heating oil options June 26, 1987	16,832 Dec. 6, 1991	142,885 Oct. 8, 1992
Natural gas options Oct. 2, 1992	2,729 Oct. 5, 1992	7,183 Oct. 9, 1992
New York Harbor gasoline options March 13, 1989	11,538 May 26, 1992	63,537 March 6, 1992
Total energy futures	276,295 Aug. 7, 1990	625,562 June 11, 1992

*As of Oct. 15, 1992.
Source: New York Mercantile Exchange

TABLE 9–2
INTERNATIONAL PETROLEUM EXCHANGE RECORDS*

Contract	Volume Date of record	Open Interest Date of record
Brent futures	66,462 Aug. 19, 1991	121,021 Aug. 7, 1990
Gas oil futures	36,058 Aug. 19, 1991	103,849 Sept. 29, 1992
Gasoline futures	1,521 June 18, 1992	5,599 July 13, 1992
Brent options	12,401 Nov. 5, 1992	70,049 Nov. 5, 1992
Gas oil options	4,579 Sept. 21, 1992	34,045 Nov. 5, 1992
Total futures	102,530 Aug. 19, 1991	203,049 Sept. 11, 1992
Total options	13,847 Oct. 30, 1992	104,094 Nov. 5, 1992
Total exchange	105,232 Aug. 19, 1991	283,725 Nov. 5, 1992

*As of Nov. 6, 1992.
Source: International Petroleum Exchange

quoted as "light, sweet crude." In addition, Nymex handles futures contracts for sour crude oil, New York Harbor unleaded gasoline, Gulf Coast unleaded gasoline, heating oil, natural gas and propane, plus a couple of nonenergy contracts. Nymex also has developed options contracts, which will be discussed later, in crude oil, heating oil, natural gas, and New York Harbor gasoline.

IPE offers futures contracts for Brent crude, gas oil (the European term for distillate-range products), naphtha, and gasoline. It handles options contracts for Brent crude and gas oil.

How
Futures
Markets
Work

Both of the key petroleum futures exchanges employ standardized contracts and open-outcry trading, which means traders meet in central locations to seek and make bids for particular contracts. Trading floors are similar to those of other commodities exchanges and to those in stock exchanges. In periods of rapid market change, the scenes become hectic.

Details about specific futures contracts are not important to analysts not planning to become traders. Nontraders should recognize that the contracts are standardized: They specify commodity or product quality and volume, and they require physical delivery of the crude or product at a specific location (in the case of Nymex) or cash settlement (in the case of IPE crude) at a certain future date.

The provision for physical delivery or cash settlement is crucial to understanding futures markets. Futures contracts trade in monthly increments into the future. A specific futures contract is identified by the delivery (or settlement) month it designates and the underlying commodity, such as July light, sweet crude. It is possible to buy or sell a contract that need not be settled until a year or more later. It is also possible to buy or sell a contract that will be settled in the following month. It is possible to resell futures contracts and to buy or sell contracts with offsetting delivery or cash settlement obligations.

As the expiration date for a futures contract approaches, the price of the contract moves toward the commodity price in the physical market. The reason is *arbitrage*—cross-trading—between the physical and futures markets. If futures prices are below physical prices $1^1/_2$ months before contract expiration, for example, refiners can buy near-month futures contracts instead of more-expensive wet barrels and hold sellers to their delivery or settlement obligations. More commonly, specialist traders called arbitrageurs seek opportunities in the price "spread" between physical and futures markets, not as a way to buy crude as cheaply as possible but as a way to earn trading profits. Arbitrage activity tends to equalize prices of wet and dry barrels as contract expirations approach; the physical and futures markets are said to converge.

The vast majority of futures contracts do not result in physical delivery of crude. Most traders discharge their contract obligations by purchasing or selling offsetting futures contracts. Thus the seller of a futures contract who does not want to have to buy or surrender wet barrels to fulfill his delivery commitments can simply buy a futures contract for the same month; the obligations cancel each other. Obviously, market conditions close to contract expiration affect these decisions.

As mentioned earlier, the IPE does not even have a provision for physical delivery of its Brent crude contract. In fact, its first Brent contract failed to gain market acceptance at least partly because it did provide for settlement in wet barrels—in amounts not representative of physical trading lots in the Brent market. In line with the successful Nymex crude contract, the first IPE contract called for delivery in 1,000 bbl lots. In the physical market, minimum volumes available fob the Brent terminal at Sullom Voe are 600,000 bbl. Moreover, the forward Brent market was well-established by the time the IPE had introduced its futures contract. Traders saw little reason to prefer the rigidities of a futures contract and exchange trading to the flexibility afforded by the already well-functioning Brent forward market. The crude futures contract IPE introduced in 1985, based as it is on cash settlement upon expiration, is more flexible and has met with far more market success.[1]

On the Nymex, too, settlement methods have become more flexible in recent years than they were at first. The exchange provides an alternate delivery procedure for buyers and sellers who notify it that they have agreed to settle in terms different from those in the standard contract. Another provision, exchange of futures for physical (EFP), enables a buyer or seller to exchange a futures position for a physical position of the same quantity upon notice to the exchange. An EFP can initiate or liquidate a futures position.

OPTIONS

fter their futures contracts became established, the exchanges introduced another type of contract that provides for more-complete hedging strategies than are available with futures contracts alone. This type of contract is called an option. It is the right to purchase or sell the underlying asset by a certain date at a certain price. It does not obligate the options owner to exercise that right. An option conveying the right to buy the underlying asset is a call. An option conveying the right to sell is a put. The seller of an option is responsible for the purchase or sale if the options buyer decides to exercise the right conveyed in the contract. Under American-style options, the option holder can exercise his buy or sell rights at any time until the contract expiration date. A European-style option can be exercised only on the expiration date.

Unlike futures contracts, options sell for premiums negotiated by the buyers and sellers, in the case of "over-the-counter" options, or via open outcry on an exchange trading floor for listed options. The price at which the option can be exercised is called the strike price. When the price of the underlying asset is above call strikes or below put strikes, the options are said to be "in the money." When the commodity price is below call strikes or above put strikes, the options are "out of the money." Obviously, an "in the money" option is more likely to be exercised than is its "out of the money" counterpart. The underlying assets for Nymex and IPE energy options are futures contracts. Thus a Nymex crude oil option represents the right to buy or sell, depending on whether it is a call or put, a Nymex crude futures contract.

Options can provide a better hedge than is available through futures contracts. In the earlier example, the trader selling futures contracts at the price he hoped to receive when he delivered his crude surrendered the possibility of earning more if prices increased beyond his expectations. He swapped what traders call upside price potential for protection against downside price risk. He could have achieved the same downside protection without giving up upside potential by buying a put with a strike price of $23/bbl—the price at which he expected to sell. For the price of the premium, he maintained the right to sell at $23/bbl no matter what happened during his cargo's voyage. But he now had no obligation to sell at $23/bbl if prices exceeded that level when his cargo reached Rotterdam. This form of hedge has its disadvantages, of course. By hedging with futures, the trader has more cash in the bank during the course of the voyage. With the options strategy, he does not recover what he paid for the cargo at Ras Tanura until he sells in Rotterdam, and he must do without the cash required for the put premium as well. Indeed, he must hope to recover the premium by selling at a price sufficiently above $23/bbl. The premium amounts to an investment in price insurance, a cost with a direct bearing on profitability.

A buyer of a put or call can dispose of the option by closing it out with an offsetting sale of the same put or call, by exercising the option, or by allowing the option to expire. The seller of a put or call is liable for performance—sale of the futures contract in the case of a Nymex call or purchase in the case of a put—if the buyer decides to exercise the option. Other than performance, the options seller escapes responsibility only by closing out the position with an offsetting options purchase or via expiration of the option.

An option's basic, or intrinsic, value is the amount by which its strike price differs from the underlying commodity price, so long as it is in the money. A crude oil put option's intrinsic value, therefore, is the amount by which its strike price exceeds the price of the corresponding crude oil futures contract. A crude call option's intrinsic value is the amount by which its strike price falls below the crude futures price. When a premium reflects value beyond the intrinsic value, the excess is called extrinsic or time value.

The main point for nontraders to remember is the difference between futures and options contracts. Futures contracts create a commitment to deliver the underlying commodity, and they trade in prices relating to those of the physical commodity itself. Options are just that: options to buy (call) or sell (put) the underlying asset at a specified price. They sell at premiums, dollars per contract rather than dollars per volume of commodity.[2]

A FEW TECHNICALITIES

t is not necessary to understand all the terms and technicalities of the paper markets in order to use them to assess petroleum-market conditions. And no attempt will be made here to probe all the complexities of this fascinating financial world. But it helps to know a few terms and basic strategies.

SHORT AND LONG

Traders can make nontraders dizzy with their jargon. Two words occur endlessly in their conversations: short and long. These are not physical descriptions. "Short" refers to the selling side of a transaction, "long" to the buying side. Traders thus talk about "going short (or long)" or "short (or long) positions." Thus, to go long, a trader can buy wet barrels, buy futures contracts, sell puts, or buy calls. To go short, a trader sells wet barrels, sells futures, sells calls, or buys puts.

THE BASIS

Another term that appears often is "basis." This usually means the difference between the price of a futures contract and that of its corresponding physical commodity. Life would be simpler for traders if the basis remained constant. The fact that it does not introduces an element of risk, called basis risk, into the simple hedge, which, to repeat, entails the simultaneous purchase of wet barrels and sale of paper barrels under a futures or forward contract. There are many reasons for the basis to change. One of them is that few wet barrel deals exactly replicate the structured, formalized transactions available in the futures market. Even for matching crudes in matching locations, wet-barrel and dry-barrel prices usually do not march precisely in step. Their trends track one another over time, but individual price movements do not; the basis changes.

Traders often quote the basis instead of absolute prices. Just as they quote specific crude values in terms of a differential against a reference crude, they cite a wet-barrel value as variation from a futures quote. Thus wet barrels of crude may be said to "trade 3 under July," which means the spot price is $3/bbl less than the latest quote for the futures contract providing for delivery or settlement in July. By concentrating on the basis, traders can earn profits no matter what wet-barrel prices do by timing their transactions to take advantage of favorable basis changes.

Other variables apply to this concept of basis. In addition to the differential between cash and futures prices for a single commodity at a single location, there is a product basis and location basis, both measured as price differences. Product basis relates to quality and grade differences between a commodity underlying a futures contract and the commodity in a related cash transaction. Location basis applies when the cash transaction will occur somewhere other than the delivery location specified in the futures contract.

VOLUME AND OPEN INTEREST

Press reports list figures for volume and open interest of futures and options contracts. Volume is the total number of transactions that occurred in the reporting period. Open interest is the total number of contracts in effect that will lead to delivery or cash settlement unless the obligations are nullified with offsetting contracts before the expiration date.

SPREADS

Traders try to profit within a single exchange from various "spreads." A typical spread is the difference between the futures price of crude and that of one or more petroleum products. Indeed, so-called "paper refiners" can approximate refining margins in the physical market with futures contract portfolios proportionate to average refining yields. In "crack spreads" such as these, crude volumes equal the sum of product volumes covered by the contracts. On Nymex, a standard portfolio is the 3-2-1 crack spread—3 bbl of crude, 2 bbl of gasoline, and 1 bbl of heating oil, which approximates U.S. refining yields. At this writing, Nymex proposed to list a crack spread contract.

There are many other types of spreads. One common type is the intramarket spread, in which a trader buys and sells a futures contract in the same commodity but in different months at a stated price differential. Also common is the intermarket spread, in which the trader "trades across the barrel"; that is, he buys and sells contracts in different energy commodities in one or more months at a stated price differential.

CONTANGO AND BACKWARDATION

The relationship between a commodity's forward or futures price and its price for immediate delivery, or prompt price, can say much about conditions in the market.

When forward or futures prices exceed the prompt price, the market is said to be in *contango*. When the prompt price exceeds the futures price, the market is in *backwardation*. These conditions exist in degrees, however. In a pure contango market, each succeeding month's futures price exceeds its predecessor, and the near-month futures price exceeds the spot price for the same commodity, although they should be converging. The reverse is true for a market in pure backwardation. When market conditions are in flux there may for a time be no clear pattern.

A contango market in which price increments between progressively distant months approximate monthly inventory carrying charges is usually considered "normal." A backwardated market, or a contango market not fully reflecting inventory carrying charges, is "inverted."[3] These terms can be misleading, however, because, as will be discussed later, some experts do not consider a contango market to be "normal" at all.

VOLATILITY

In futures and options markets, analysts often discuss "volatility," a term discussed earlier. A workable, nontechnical definition of this term might be the market's relative changeability. Analysts measure volatility by ranking past prices and determining an average variation from the price holding the middle position in the list—the median price.

There are two main types of volatility. Historical volatility measures past price movements. Implied volatility measures expected price movements. Volatility is an important determinant of options premiums. Options values usually move in line with market volatility: the greater the volatility, the higher the options value. The options market can function, therefore, as a gauge of market volatility.

It is not a perfect gauge, however. Other factors in options values must be taken into account, especially time remaining until expiration. Generally, the more time an option has until expiration, the greater is its value. A rising premium for a particular option, therefore, may result more from simple maturation than from rising market volatility. What the analyst must watch to test volatility is premiums for, say, three months' forward options over time, rather than the premium of a particular month's option as it progresses toward expiration.

SWAPS

Oil and gas producers sometimes use a financial tool called the swap to hedge their future production streams. It involves an over-the-counter exchange of cash flows with a trading *counterparty*, according to a negotiated formula involving a fixed price and floating price.

The producer enters the swap for protection against price declines. The protection comes from the fixed price in the swap contract. The counterparty, usually a trading company, enters the swap in hopes of benefiting from future price increases beyond the fixed price in the swap contract.

A swap contract might call for monthly settlement for a year's worth of production. On a certain day of each month, the producer receives cash from the counterparty equal to the fixed price times a specified reference quantity of production. In turn, the producer pays the counterparty an amount equal to the floating price—the current market price according to some agreed indicator, such as the near-month futures price—times the reference quantity. This payment to the counterparty should come close to the revenues the producer earns on physical sales of his production, or that portion of production equal to the reference quantity in the swaps contract.

The swap, then, is purely a financial transaction—an exchange of cash flows—that a producer arranges as protection against downside price risk. It works parallel to the cash flows he receives from actual production.

DERIVATIVES

Swaps, futures, and options belong to a family of risk management tools called "derivatives." These are trading instruments that in some way take the place of the commodity they represent. Derivatives markets develop over time. Officials of the formal exchanges launch new futures and options contracts as opportunities arise. The over-the-counter market is even more fluid. Derivative forms evolve continually and will continue to do so as investors seek new ways to manage risks and seek trading profits.

FUTURES AND INVENTORIES

ithout doubt, paper-barrel markets represent an important, relatively new dimension of the oil market. They offer protection against the risks of price changes to people who need to own crude but who do not want to gamble on price movements. They create the opportunity for speculative trading profits for people who are willing to assume price risks but have no reason to own oil. And they give the market a real-time view of what prices are doing. Prices in most physical market contracts now usually are keyed in some way to the futures price of comparable crudes or products.

Paper barrels, however, do not burn. A refiner cannot process a crude-oil futures contract. Motorists do not buy gasoline calls at service stations.

Nothing about the forward and futures markets reduces the need for movement of petroleum through the containment system that constitutes the physical market. More particularly, nothing about the paper markets reduces the need for physical inventories capable of smoothing transportation and processing timing discrepancies and of accommodating unexpected swings in demand. The paper markets essentially give inventory owners the ability to lay off the price-associated risks of holding—or not holding—stocks. This frees inventory owners to manage stocks more in accordance with physical operational requirements and demand expectations and less in anticipation of future price changes. A refiner, for example, can buy crude for storage before a period of expected high operating rates and hedge with futures or options contracts against price declines. Indeed, this has become standard practice. A refiner also can use futures contracts to meet future crude needs in lieu of holding wet barrels in inventory, but this is not nearly as common a refiner practice as hedging is.

Like everything else in the market, however, the practice of building and hedging stocks has limits in addition to those relating to storage capacity. If all refiners decide to buy wet barrels for storage and sell paper barrels for price protection, what happens to prices? Wet-barrel prices rise because of the inherent boost in immediate demand, and paper-barrel prices sag because of the increase in supply represented by all those refiners offering to sell futures contracts. With the immediate price of wet barrels—the prompt price—now higher than the futures price, the market is in backwardation.

Refiners' motivations shift in response. Backwardation means a refiner cannot sell paper barrels at a price affording full downside protection against the prompt price for physical barrels. There is a school of thought that says refiners will accept some forward discount from the prompt price as the cost of insurance against future price declines. According to this view, backwardation is the normal condition of the market. Refiners seem to have other ideas. The market is in backwardation some of the time and contango at other times, with changes that seem to be associated with changes in inventory levels.[4]

Indeed, why should refiners pay for insurance when they do not have to? Buying dear wet barrels for storage and selling cheap paper barrels for partial price protection makes no sense. At some point in a backwardated market refiners will quit buying wet barrels for storage and start buying paper barrels with delivery or cash settlement times corresponding to their operating needs.

For these reasons, in this author's view, there is nothing "normal" about a backwardated market, even though markets for some commodities in some locations may be in backwardation more than they are in contango. Backwardation is an incentive not to hold stocks. There are times when that is, indeed, the proper incentive to be at work in the market. Normally, however, the market—thanks to the concern of every participant for future supply—wants a surplus. As earlier chapters have argued, the market pays for the maintenance of a production capacity surplus in the form of high economic rents to producers with the lowest operating costs. Similarly, everything else being in relative balance, the market will pay for maintenance of inventories somewhat beyond operating requirements in the form of a futures premium to the prompt price of oil: a contango. It always costs more for a supplier in the oil market to be caught short than it does to have too much for sale. Protection against price surprise is important; protection against shortage is more so. If anything, therefore, the market should tend toward contango.

Here, then, is another assertion that strays from accepted economic wisdom. But it may prove more useful than orthodox explanations are to the economic layperson trying to understand market movements. Economists usually describe contango as a reflection of carrying costs of oil in storage or an implicit return on the investment made in stored oil. The problem arises in trying to measure all the economic variables involved in that explanation while a market correction is in progress. Events seem to bear out the theory, but precise measurements must be made in retrospect, after it is too late to use the prompt-futures price relationship as an analytical tool.

What the practical analyst must remember is that futures prices are related to inventory levels, the desirable level of which is always difficult to ascertain. A market in contango—in which futures contracts trade at a premium to prompt barrels—is creating incentives to hold crude in storage if the premium is sufficient to offset carrying costs. A market in backwardation is creating incentives to liquidate inventories. A swing from one condition to another is a sure sign that something has changed in the oil market, which may or may not be apparent at the time of the shift.

Prices in the paper-barrel markets, then, represent something more than traders' best guesses about physical markets—although they certainly are that. They influence, and are influenced by, real volumes of oil in storage. The analyst should remain alert to changes in the relationship between prompt and forward prices and in inventory levels. All the variables interact. Changes may result from something dramatic, such as an interruption somewhere in the supply chain. Or they may stem from something more subtle, such as collective decisions by refiners that last year's oil inventories amounted to three days too much in terms of forward consumption.

The essence of analysis is being able to interpret current

trends, however subtle, and to correctly anticipate the market's next move (or two). For this, information available from the futures markets has become indispensable.

REFERENCES

1. Mabro, Robert, Bacon, Robert, Chadwick, Margaret, Halliwell, Mark, Long, David, *The Market for North Sea Crude Oil*, Oxford Institute for Energy Studies, Oxford University Press, 1986.

2. O'Connell, John H., *Petroleum Options Newsletter*, Refco Inc., New York, various issues, 1986–87. Much of the material on options comes from this source.

3. *Glossary of Petroleum and Commodity Futures Industry Terms*, New York Mercantile Exchange.

4. "Forward and Futures Markets and Oil Price Stability," *Global Oil Report*, Vol. 2, No. 2, Centre for Global Energy Studies, March-April, 1991.

CHAPTER TEN

FINDING
THE
INFORMATION

The three questions fundamental to oil market analysis have many dimensions. Demand depends on economic activity, prices, investments in technology to improve energy use efficiency, weather conditions, politics, and other factors. Supply depends on prices, investment in production and processing capacities, decisions about utilization of spare capacities, and other factors. Price depends on the ever-changing relationships between supply and demand. To answer the fundamental market questions, the analyst must piece together information from enough sources to construct a meaningful picture of conditions. With petroleum futures trading so much a part of the modern market, and with computers disseminating information with ever-increasing speed and volume, finding pertinent market data is not a problem. The challenge is to make sense of all the numbers.

Approaching the oil market in terms of the three basic questions about demand, supply, and price can help cut through the tangle of statistics on important operations, such as production. This production scene is in Harris County, Texas, just west of Houston.

Price information is everywhere. To some extent this has always been so. Service stations, after all, have always advertised gasoline prices on huge signs in most parts of the world. Price information for other petroleum products has been nearly as easy to acquire. Until the spot market, later joined by the futures exchanges, came to dominate trading, crude prices were less visible.

Now, however, prices for crude are as accessible as those for products. There are still private term contracts for crude oil, to be sure. But prices in those deals are nearly always linked to a futures or spot price that anyone can see. No one any longer questions whether spot and forward markets accurately represent the market, as some did when the paper markets were developing. For all practical purposes, spot and forward markets are the modern petroleum market.

The question thus is no longer whether accurate price information is available but rather what form it needs to take to suit particular needs. Traders obviously need price information as close to real time as they can get it. They all subscribe to computer reporting services that track futures-market transactions as they occur and keep tabs on physical markets as well. Nontraders usually do not need nearly instantaneous information of that type. In fact, price movements during the course of a trading day or week often can be misleading. Rumors of political problems in an important oil-producing country might make crude futures prices jump $3/bbl one hour, only to be proven untrue the next, perhaps replaced by pessimistic reports—yet to be substantiated—about economic activity and therefore petroleum demand in Europe. Traders need to react to every bit of news that might affect petroleum markets, and they do. But much such news turns out not to be fact, in which cases traders react in the opposite directions.

More useful to nontrading analysts are data that show price trends rather than individual movements. Market newsletters provide this type of information. The most important of them probably are McGraw-Hill's Platt's series of price and market reports, *Petroleum Intelligence Weekly,* and *Petroleum Argus,* although there are others that do credible jobs of keeping up with petroleum markets. The newsletters cited here provide good price information as well as useful analysis about market trends. Each has its specialty. In addition to reporting basic price data, the newsletters usually derive important market indicators, such as crude-oil netback values, from the raw information.

Price and market information also appears to varying degrees in trade magazines such as *Oil & Gas Journal, Petroleum Economist, World Oil,* and *Oil & Gas Investor.* These journals—all monthly except for the weekly *Oil & Gas Journal*—focus on varying nonmarket aspects of the petroleum business but can provide useful historic data, spot critical market trends, and remain reasonably up to date.

NEWSPAPER PRICE REPORTS

Daily basic price information is available in financial newspapers and, to some degree, in the metropolitan newspapers of cities in oil-producing or refining regions. Regional spot price information is usually available at least for crude, heating oil, and gasoline. The data are easy to understand, often simply a quote for a transaction at some time during the preceding day and one for a transaction at the same time the day before that.

Newspapers that print spot prices usually publish futures prices as well. Formats for futures quotes are slightly more complicated than those for spot prices. The individual petroleum categories—crude and the various products—are, of course, reported separately. Under each commodity category are lines for months into the future, as far ahead as contracts are available on the exchange. Each month represents a separately traded contract. Most formats report four prices for each contract: open, high, low, and settle. The open price covers the day's first transaction. The high and low prices show the price range within which the contract traded during the day. And the settle figure is the price at the end of the trading day. There usually is a change column showing the difference between that day's settle price and the settle price of the preceding trading day. On the Nymex, crude quotes are in dollars per barrel, product quotes in cents per gallon. Sales and open interest figures also appear in each commodity category. The sales figure shows the number of transactions during the trading day. The open interest figure is the number of outstanding contracts.

Options reporting formats differ from those for futures. Each horizontal line in an options report represents a strike price identified in the left column, often preceded by the settle price of the underlying futures contract to show the spread. To the right of the strike price appear six figures, the premiums for calls three months into the future and those for puts three months forward.

From newspapers that report these basic market data, then, the analyst can learn much. Spot and near-month futures contract quotes give the best indication of current values for crude and products. Comparison of those values with recent quotes shows trends.

In addition, a comparison of the spot with futures prices and of near-month with distant futures values shows whether the market is in contango or backwardation. This determination offers clues about inventory tendencies. A sudden change from contango to backwardation or vice versa can signal a significant market shift, which may or may not already be apparent.

Options price trends can signal changes in market volatility, since premiums rise with volatility. But other factors must be taken into account, such as interest rates and times until expiration. Premiums shrink as expiration dates approach, everything else remaining the same.

The analyst can use spot and futures prices to estimate refining margins, using a crack spread calculation such as the one described in Chapter 4 and plugging in estimates of transportation and operating costs. Product yield assumptions are important in these calculations, of course. For complex refineries in the United States, yields of 60% gasoline and 40% fuel oil can be assumed. Some analysts use the "3-2-1" crack spread formula, which is about the same thing: 3 bbl of crude, 2 bbl of gasoline, and 1 bbl of heating oil. In other parts of the world, refineries make proportionately less gasoline. In Japan, for example, the more typical spread is 60% heating oil and 40% gasoline. Refining margin trends are important. Crude price increases in conjunction with margin growth reflect market strength; refiners are able to pass along the higher feedstock costs, which means product demand is strong. On the other hand, crude price increases that shrink or wipe out refining margins cannot last long without taking their toll in processing capacity.

SUPPLY
AND
DEMAND
INFORMATION

Nonprice market information is usually only slightly more difficult than price data to find. Sources vary country by country. Most governments publish information of this type through petroleum ministries, state oil companies, or energy agencies. Petroleum market newsletters and trade magazines publish the information as it is available.

The most important demand information comes from the United States. This is partly because this country is the world's single largest petroleum consuming nation. It also is because United States market data influence futures contract prices on the Nymex, which in turn influence prices worldwide.

In the United States, the most important market data come from two sources. One is the federal Department of Energy's Energy Information Administration (EIA). EIA publishes a series of market periodicals tracking supply, demand, prices, and some industry operating data. EIA also provides annual estimates of U.S. crude oil and natural gas reserves.

The other main source of U.S. market data is the American Petroleum Institute (API). The trade association publishes a monthly formal market report that includes, among other things, an estimate of U.S. consumption based on deliveries from primary storage, total and product by product. The report also covers production and other indicators of supply and is probably the best gauge of the U.S. petroleum market.

API also publishes weekly statistics on U.S. crude oil and product inventories, imports, and refinery operations. These numbers move markets. API releases the figures each Tuesday, after the Nymex has closed, and futures prices on Wednesday often change based on what the API numbers show. Traders pay special attention to inventory figures. A stocks surprise on Tuesday evening usually produces a noticeable price change on Wednesday morning.

Immediate price movements such as these usually do not mean much. A broad understanding of the market comes from more than price zigs and zags. The API numbers, and comparable figures that may be available in other countries, should be examined in the context of several weeks' or even months' worth of history. Looked at in this way, the numbers can show:

1. Trends in spare processing capacity. Is the utilization rate increasing or decreasing? Is the change a result of rising crude runs or decreasing capacity or some combination of these factors?

2. Whether feedstock is coming from storage, which would be indicated by a decline in crude stocks, or from direct purchases, reflected in steady or increasing crude inventories at a time of increasing crude runs.

3. Whether product is moving to market or accumulating in inventories. The key indicators here are product inventories and consumption (deliveries from primary inventories, in the API reports).

4. Sources of supply: Domestic production and imports of crude oil and products.

5. Whether foreign product is undercutting domestic refinery

output, which would appear as an increase in product imports and decline in refinery throughput and capacity utilization.

6. Days' supply of crude, product, and total (crude plus product) inventories, calculated by dividing current stock levels by current consumption.

Price information should supplement analyses like these. An increase in refining capacity utilization might be a response to high margins. Or refiners might be making product for storage if inventories have dropped to low levels, in which case prices theoretically should be adjusting in order to widen margins and provide the incentive to increase crude runs—but may not be.

Regional numbers say much. They provide a solid feel for market conditions and an understanding of current price movements. For the reasons cited earlier, the API and EIA standard data are especially important in the United States and around the world. Trade publications and financial newspapers usually report the information regularly. Interpreting these widely available statistics should become habitual practice for anyone wanting to follow the oil market's patterns and changes.

WORLDWIDE ANALYSIS

 till, the API and EIA reports do not fully answer the three key market questions:

1. How much oil does the world need?

2. How much oil can (or will) the world deliver to market? and

3. How do the answers to the first two questions affect, and

how are they affected by, price?

A convenient single source has developed for information essential to the answers. It is the *Monthly Oil Market Report* of the International Energy Agency. The IEA formed after the Arab oil embargo to, among other things, administer emergency oil-sharing agreements among industrialized, oil-consuming countries. It is an agency of the Organization for Economic Cooperation and Development (OECD), representing the 25 nations commonly thought to constitute the industrialized world. In addition to 18 nations in Europe and Scandinavia, OECD members include the United States, Canada, Japan, Australia, and New Zealand. All OECD members except Sweden and the former Yugoslavia belong to IEA.

The *Monthly Oil Market Report,* which IEA offers on a subscription basis, contains detailed worldwide data on production, demand, prices, and stocks. Its contents are reported widely in the petroleum press.

While the report contains a great volume and variety of information, one page deserves and receives special attention. It is a table entitled "World Oil Supply and Demand," generically a "global balance" table. IEA's global balance and similar tables from other sources are standard tools of petroleum economics and mainstays of oil market reporting and analysis.

IEA's global balance table arranges data types along a vertical scale and times, in quarters and years, along a horizontal scale (Table 10–1). Values are in millions of barrels per day.

There are three main categories of data types, arranged along the vertical scale: demand, supply, and stock change and miscellaneous. Demand and supply are subdivided regionally. Demand is

TABLE 10–1
FORMAT OF A WIDELY REPORTED GLOBAL OIL BALANCE*

DEMAND
OECD
      America
      Europe
      Pacific
      TOTAL OECD
NON-OECD
      USSR
      China
      Europe
      Latin America
      Asia
      Middle East
      Africa
      TOTAL NON-OECD
TOTAL DEMAND

SUPPLY
      OECD
      USSR
      China
      Other non-OPEC
      Processing Gains
      TOTAL NON-OPEC
OPEC
      Crude
      NGLs
      TOTAL OPEC
TOTAL SUPPLY

STOCK CHANGE AND MISCELLANEOUS
REPORTED OECD
      Industry
      Government
      TOTAL OECD
      Floating Storage/Oil in Transit
      Other & Misc. to balance
TOTAL STOCK CHANGE AND MISCELLANEOUS

*Data categories from the World Oil Supply and Demand table in
International Energy Agency's *Monthly Oil Market Report.* Data are historic by quarters for current year quarters and preceding two years, plus
annual for the year before them. IEA projects demand and non-OPEC
supply by quarter for four quarters forward. Analysts must make assumptions about stock changes and OPEC NGL production to calculate the
"call on OPEC" crude production. Global oil balances from most other
sources resemble this one.

divided among the OECD and non-OECD segments of the world, each segment further divided into key countries or regions.

The principal supply categories are OPEC and non-OPEC. Supply is measured as production of crude oil, condensates, natural gas liquids, and nonconventional oil, plus non-OPEC processing gains. Processing gains, typically adding 1.4 million B/D to non-OPEC supply, reflect chemical changes that crude undergoes in refining: As molecules are rearranged and other substances, mainly hydrogen, are added, petroleum gains volume without commensurate gains in weight. The stock changes are rates of inventory buildup or drawdown in OECD nations, estimates of changes elsewhere and in floating storage and transit, and a balancing estimate to make supply equal demand.

In the supply and demand table, IEA projects demand and non-OPEC production forward for several quarters. Projections in these areas are usually fairly straightforward. An examination of recent worldwide demand trends and some assumptions about economic growth in the next several quarters provide a solid basis for demand forecasts. And production outside of OPEC members is readily predictable as well. With minor exceptions, non-OPEC producing nations produce at capacity. Their current production can be projected forward and adjusted for natural declines and increases resulting from new fields due on stream in the forecast period or production growth from known enhanced recovery or drilling projects.

The wild card is OPEC production, which reflects the group's decisions about quotas and individual members' adherence to those decisions. The usual use of the IEA supply and demand table, and other such global balance representations, is to solve for the OPEC production variable. First, something must be assumed for stock changes. Economists often simply remove inventories from the equation by assuming no change at all. It is possible to examine historic stock data and seasonal patterns and insert some reasonable value about what may happen in future quarters with stocks. Assuming no change at least makes things simple.

An assumption about OPEC production of NGL follows the assumption about stocks. For the most part, OPEC excludes NGL production from its quotas. NGL output is a function of gas rather than oil production and thus can be assumed to fall outside of the scope of OPEC decisions and politics. In fact, NGLs find their ways into OPEC export cargoes and may or may not be counted as crude oil production. For purposes of worldwide supply, however, OPEC NGL production can safely be assumed to fall within a narrow range of 1.9–2 million B/D, regardless of quotas, and be counted separately from crude.

At this point, the analysis has projected or made assumptions about world demand, providing a contingent answer to the first principal question of petroleum market analysis. It has projected or made assumptions about the reasonably stable factors of world supply, providing a contingent answer to the part of the second question relating to how much oil the world can deliver to market. What remains is to establish the market's need for that most discretional of supply factors, the answer to the "will" part of the second question, OPEC crude production. Since supply must equal demand, simple arithmetic provides the answer. Projected demand minus projected and assumed supply other than OPEC crude output leaves what is known as the call on OPEC. It is the rate at which OPEC must make crude oil available in order to balance the market. And it is crucial because it represents the physical margin of supply.

The analyst must compare this call on OPEC crude against several values:

1. Current production. Will OPEC have to increase or decrease production in future quarters?

2. The OPEC quota. Has OPEC set its quota accurately, aligning it with the best available estimates for the call on its members' crude? If not, how will discrepancies be resolved? Or can they be?

3. OPEC production capacity. Can members, in fact, produce enough to satisfy the market's call on their crude?

The relationship between the derived call on OPEC crude and these values is crucial to crude-oil values. It is normal for OPEC production capacity to exceed current production and the call on OPEC crude; the market usually is in surplus. OPEC, therefore, usually faces the difficult chore of producing an agreement among its members on a group quota and on individual quotas within the total. Members want to produce as much as they can but do not want prices to suffer, which means they want others to restrain output. In order to come to accord, the group sometimes makes overly optimistic assumptions about the call on its crude and thus sets a group quota significantly above more-reasonable call projections.

Sometimes, however, usually after interruptions of flow from important non-OPEC producers or OPEC capacity reductions such as those resulting from export embargoes, group capacity can appear inadequate in relation to the market's call on group crude production. So-called price hawks might even have their way and somehow succeed in setting and enforcing a group quota below what the market needs.

Anticipated deviations from the call on OPEC crude provide much of the answer to the third basic oil-market question (how supply and demand affect, and are affected by, prices). An OPEC quota set too high, or production in excess of a reasonable quota, manifests surplus and depresses prices. A quota set too low or an insufficiency of capacity has the opposite effect. Eventually and inevitably, the price responses to these deviations alter the course of supply and demand and move the market toward balance at some new level of each.

Indeed, useful as IEA's supply and demand table is, the values change with time. Very properly, the agency adjusts its demand projections from quarter to quarter to reflect the market's changes.

There are variations to the IEA global balance, all designed to rectify weaknesses assumed to hamper the IEA approach. Some analysts, for example, seek a more precise measure of demand for crude than IEA can provide. Their aim is to better correlate crude prices with crude demand. IEA's demand figures reflect product consumption as measured by deliveries from identifiable storage. Product consumption worldwide exceeds crude production if stocks do not change, especially when the measurements are volumetric. There are two main explanations for this. One is that refinery output contains substances besides crude oil, such as NGLs, hydrogen, ethers, and alcohols, which are added during processing and that add weight and volume. The other is that refining processes rearrange the molecules in crude oil in such a way that they would end up taking more space even if they did not gain weight with the addition of noncrude inputs. Altogether, refinery streams grow more in volume than they do in weight during blending and processing. The added volumes are refining or processing gains.

It would seem that subtracting processing gains and all identifiable NGL production from a global oil balance such as IEA's would leave a rough approximation of demand for crude. But there is another complication related to timing. Current product consumption is based on crude produced and purchased days, weeks, or months ago. The analyst needing to correlate crude prices with crude demand needs a more-current representation of crude demand than the one that can be derived from product demand. One analyst, Energy Security Analysis Inc. of Washington, D.C., tries to resolve the timing problem by measuring crude demand or purchases for strategic storage, plus direct burn of crude (800,000 to 1 million B/D worldwide), plus refinery throughput.[1] Other analysts no doubt find problems with the approach, but it illustrates an important subtlety of petroleum economic analysis.

Whatever the approach, supply and demand must balance. It is in the adjustment process necessary to effect that balance that the analyst sees what really is happening in the market and finds the answer, if one is necessary, to the question: Where's the shortage?

REFERENCES

1. Emerson, Sara A., Energy Security Analysis Inc., presentation to first annual Stockwatch Seminar, Houston, March 19, 1993.

CHAPTER ELEVEN

THE MARKET AND WAR

Use your imagination for a moment. Place yourself in the oil market, anywhere in the closed system that this book has described, downstream of the wellhead and upstream of the retail pump. No matter where you choose, you buy and sell petroleum in some form, either to process it or to trade or distribute it for profit.

So you have sales commitments. Let us say those commitments add up to 10,000 B/D. Your business is solid, in part because your customers consider you a reliable supplier. You make a good living.

It is the second day of August, 1990. The telephone rings. It

Two years after the retreat of Iraqi troops from Kuwait, remnants of war still littered the Kuwaiti desert. This is a destroyed Iraqi tank. Behind it, a Kuwait Santa Fe drilling rig repairs a well in northern Kuwait's Raudhatain oil field.

is your best customer.

"Can I rely on you?" he asks, panic in his voice.

You are confused. "Of course—"

"Didn't you hear?"

"What are you talking about?"

"Iraq just invaded Kuwait. One of my suppliers just called,

said he was relying on a tanker cargo due out of Mina Abdulla in 10 days, only Mina Abdulla's closed. I need an extra 2,000 bbl a day. I'm counting on you."

You are honest. "I didn't know about this thing in Iraq. I'll have to check my suppliers—"

"I'm in a jam. I'll pay spot plus two bucks a barrel."

Spot plus two? You have a built-in margin. "I'll get back to you in an hour," you say.

Of course you cannot short your other customers, all of whom call within the hour, in order to deliver the extra 2,000 B/D. And you worry about the 10,000 bbl a day you regularly receive.

You hit the phones. Crude was selling at $18/bbl on the Rotterdam spot market before the Iraqi invasion. Now buyers everywhere are worried.

That some upset was imminent in the Middle East was obvious. Before he sent troops into Kuwait, Iraqi President Saddam Hussein had bullied members of the Organization of Petroleum Exporting Countries into an untenable agreement. Unable to support export prices of $18/bbl, OPEC nevertheless agreed to a target price $3/bbl higher and a second-half production ceiling 400,000 B/D higher than its predecessor.

So what does Saddam want in Kuwait? To balance the market by forcibly removing nearly 2 million B/D of Kuwaiti production from the market? To expropriate Kuwaiti production and make his money on volume and not worry about prices? To continue his march southward and capture the biggest oil prize of all, Saudi Arabia?

No one knows. What you know is that you have commitments to deliver your regular 10,000 B/D of petroleum plus 2,000 B/D more to keep your best customer happy. You quickly learn that your own suppliers have more than the usual numbers of competing bids.

If you want to stay in business, if you want to maintain your reputation as a reliable supplier, you must induce your suppliers to sell to you and not to your competitors. And you have one way to do that: Make the highest bid for each cargo of crude you seek.

RATIONAL PHENOMENON

What's happening here?

The answer is simple, the phenomenon altogether rational. With excellent reason, the oil market perceived Iraq's invasion of Kuwait as a serious threat to supply. Saddam Hussein raised fears of everyone in the market about that premier concern: replacement supply.

So prices rose.

By Monday, August 6, the New York Mercantile Exchange price of a futures contract for September delivery of light, sweet crude had reached $28.05/bbl, up $3.56 from the preceding Friday—the day after the invasion—and up $8.27 from the preceding Monday. The spot price of Brent blend jumped to $25.90/bbl on August 7 from $19.45/bbl the week before.

The political response was immediate. "Uncertainties in the Middle East pose no immediate threat to the supply of petroleum products for American consumers," soothed the U.S. Department of Energy. "Nor do they necessitate increases in prices for

American consumers."

Imagine yourself in the oil market again, not knowing how much oil the invasion would remove from the market, not knowing whether Saudi Arabia would be affected, pressured by your customers to keep supplies moving. How would you have reacted to the DOE pronouncement?

Even as the department issued its blithe market assurances, President George Bush was knitting together the international coalition that eventually would crush the Iraqi occupying force and at least contain Saddam Hussein's ability to pursue military mischief in the Persian Gulf region. Bush did not go to all that trouble simply to teach Saddam a lesson. He went to the trouble, he placed American lives at risk, precisely because the "uncertainties" generated by the Iraqi leader posed the "immediate threat to the supply of petroleum products" that the DOE was denying. This, in fact, constitutes very good reason for prices to increase. With one important exception, everyone concerned about replacement oil supply, everyone concerned about keeping petroleum flowing through the closed system from wellhead to gasoline pump, understood this simple fact of market life. The exception was the ultimate consumer, who had to try to make sense out of what was happening on the basis of absurd utterances such as that from the DOE.

Alas, DOE was not the only office, public or private, to get things wrong. The U.S. Department of Justice, prodded by attorneys general from several states, began an immediate antitrust investigation into oil companies' pricing behavior—an investigation that, long after the market had returned to normal, would find no reason to prosecute anyone. Oil companies, in fact, took steps to freeze prices at wholesale and retail levels in the weeks after the invasion. It was a well-intentioned strategy that would backfire when similar responses to the outbreak of hostilities the following January would become floors instead of ceilings. The market eventually made everyone look dumb.

Despite oil companies' efforts to blunt the effects of the market interruption on consumers, gasoline prices did jump, although not by nearly as much as crude prices did. As usual, politicians took advantage of this understandably unpopular but altogether foreseeable outcome. Lawmakers introduced bills to reinstate the "windfall profit" tax on oil. Democratic Senator Richard Bryan of Nevada later would make a statement that typified much official response to the market's reaction to the invasion: "In the days immediately after the invasion the big oil companies lost no time in running up prices. There was no shortage of oil to justify such a rapid rise in the price of gasoline." The theme would echo throughout the world, even in the International Energy Agency, which keeps such close track of international market developments and plays such a pivotal role in triggering emergency withdrawals from strategic inventories. In late October, Ulrich Engelmann, IEA board chairman, observed that there was no oil shortage but that the system was running at capacity.

By then, Iraq's invasion and an international embargo had removed 4.3 million B/D of crude oil and products from the market, which in turn was staging a classic adjustment to a severe upset. And the best that the official world could do was ask: Where's the shortage?

A
CLASSIC
ADJUSTMENT

The Iraqi invasion of Kuwait and retaliatory economic embargo of the invader and victim did, indeed, create a shortage. But it was shortage to the only extent that shortage can occur in a freely functioning, closed market. That is, supply did become the principal constraint, and price and demand adjusted accordingly. The adjustment occurred where everyone could see it and was accurately reflected and reported in IEA's own *Monthly Oil Market Report*. Yet officialdom kept up its futile hunt for what can never be found in a closed market: physical shortage, sudden and surprising void, as though market participants were supposed never to recognize supply jeopardy and respond rationally to it.

It is true that stocks were full when Iraq invaded Kuwait. Persistent quota violations by Kuwait in the face of ample supply— and consequent price declines—probably helped provoke the invasion in the first place. For its part, Kuwait saw low oil prices as a way to deprive Iraq of the revenues essential to its massive arms buildup. Long fearful of aggression from its northern neighbor, Kuwait viewed rapid reconstruction of the Iraqi military after its devastating eight-year engagement with Iran as an immediate threat. Events of August 2, 1990, ratified the Kuwaiti perception. Historians eventually will note the irony here: Kuwait was exercising its only defense, overproducing its quota to weaken oil prices and thereby to keep money out of Saddam Hussein's hands. In doing so, it probably drove the Iraqi dictator to such financial desperation that he had little to lose in launching the invasion—so long as he thought, as he apparently did, that the United States and other major oil consuming nations would not respond. Saddam's mistake, of course, made his conquest short-lived and cost the lives of hundreds of thousands of his country's soldiers. And Kuwait's preinvasion overproduction, an act of self-preservation matched for competitive reasons by other OPEC members, had poured oil into storage.

In the first quarter of 1990, according to IEA estimates, onshore stocks in member countries of the Organization for Economic Cooperation and Development increased at an average rate of 800,000 B/D.[1] In the second quarter, stocks built at an average rate of 500,000 B/D. Most of the buildup was in company stocks in Europe and North America. The reason for the stock build was, of course, OPEC overproduction, largely a reflection of Kuwaiti quota busting. July production averaged 23.2 million B/D. IEA at the time was projecting a third quarter call on OPEC crude of 1 million B/D less than what OPEC was producing. This is why OPEC's July agreement to raise its target price by $3/bbl and to increase a mostly ignored group quota made so little sense.

Thus, in the month before the invasion, OECD stocks on land represented 99 days of forward consumption, high by historic standards and a full three days more than the preceding year. The inventory cushion certainly helped the market adjust to loss of Kuwaiti and Iraqi exports. And, of course, it gave politicians something to point at during their sanctimonious railings against price jumps.

A stock cushion, however, is just that: a cushion. As we have seen, not all inventories are accessible, even though inaccessible, nonworking volumes usually count toward coverage of forward consumption. And of the volumes in OECD inventories in July, a total of 590 million bbl lay in strategic storage in the United States and 425 million bbl in government stocks elsewhere in the OECD. Immediately after the Iraqi invasion, no one in the market knew the conditions under which that oil would become available.

It must be remembered—and it should have been noted by officials at the time—that market participants must constantly concern themselves with replacement supply. No one knew how long Iraqi and Kuwaiti oil would be off the market. Everyone feared for Saudi production. No matter how high inventories are at any time, they simply provide breathing room between an interruption in continuous flow through the market's closed system and startup of continuous flow from new or idle sources replacing what was lost. In the Persian Gulf crisis, commercial inventories performed the task well. But they were just one part of a much broader market adjustment.

Few took accurate account of this adjustment while it was under way. Officials kept up their rhetorical hunt for physical shortage until the very end of the crisis. Oil companies made their embarrassing price freezes when allied forces began their rout of Iraqi troops in January 1991. IEA waited until the market had completed its adjustment and had rendered additional supply altogether unnecessary before releasing oil from government stocks.

There is a good reason for this wholesale misreading of the market. No one had ever seen the oil market respond to a crisis of these proportions in the absence of price and usage controls in the principal consuming countries. The oil market responded to the

Persian Gulf crisis precisely as a free market should to a sudden cutoff of a significant portion of supply. Apparently, many government and oil company officials still harbored antiquated doubts that the law of supply and demand applies to petroleum. The Persian Gulf crisis should dispel those doubts forever.

A
REVIEW

 review of this classic market adjustment is, therefore, in order. In capsule form, here is what happened: Invasion of one of the world's most important oil producers and threats to another, even more important producer, elevated market fears about replacement supply. Prices increased. In response to the higher prices, idle production capacity came on stream and supplies came forward from new sources. Also in response to higher prices, demand fell. Within a few months, the market had regained confidence in stability of the new balance of supply, demand, and price. Fears about replacement supply subsided. Once it became clear, through Iraq's surprisingly weak response to allied attack, that Saudi oil fields would not come to harm, the market signaled, through a price drop, that it did not need Iraqi and Kuwaiti oil at all to meet demand anticipated in the following few quarters.

This is how the market is supposed to work. Leaders of consuming nation countries deserve credit for letting it happen, for not slapping price or consumption controls onto oil products as they had in previous crises. The fact remains that the process of market adjustment was becoming clear within weeks of the Iraqi invasion. All anyone had to do to understand what was going on was to ask the three basic market questions: How much oil does the world need? How much oil can (or will) the world make available to the market? And how do the answers to the first two questions interact with one another and with price? The answers, as always, were available in regularly published data.

Because of the concern for replacement supply, today's market changes come in response to changes in expectations about tomorrow's consumption and supply. So the crucial demand figures are always those relating to future periods. As Chapter 10 showed, useful demand projections appear in IEA's *Oil Market Report*, from which the call on OPEC crude can be calculated.

In its report for the end of July 1990, IEA was projecting consumption outside the centrally planned economies of 52.6 million B/D for the third quarter. Apparently anticipating hoarding, IEA the following month raised its third-quarter demand projection to 53.1 million B/D. For the fourth quarter, however, the projection reversed. A fourth-quarter projection of 55.3 million B/D made at the end of July dropped to 54.5 million B/D at the end of August. The numbers, of course, changed during the course of the crisis, as we shall see. The important point here is that IEA very properly was anticipating some slump in demand as a consequence of elevated prices.

Attention early in the crisis, however, focused on replacing the Iraqi and Kuwaiti crude and products lost to international trade. The volumes amounted to about 4.3 million B/D. In September, it was believed that Saudi Arabia might be able to raise production by 2 million B/D, Venezuela by 500,000 B/D, and other OPEC members by 700,000 B/D. Those volumes add up to

3.2 million B/D, leaving a shortfall in excess of 1 million B/D to come from stocks and production increases outside of OPEC. In many news reports during the period, this was not seen as much of a challenge. In fact, however, this is a lot to ask of stocks, and new production materializes only when there is an inducement in the form of price increases.

The market, of course, provided the inducement. In August, immediately after the invasion, it looked forward to that 55.3 million B/D of free-world demand IEA was projecting for the fourth quarter and asked, How much can (or will) the world produce? It was reasonable and prudent at the time to assume that production outside OPEC and the centrally planned economies was at capacity. In its end-July report, IEA estimated non-OPEC supply at 28.4 million B/D. Most spare production capacity was correctly thought to exist within OPEC. The remaining key variable, therefore, was OPEC capacity to produce without Iraq and Kuwait.

The U.S. Central Intelligence Agency before the crisis estimated available OPEC crude oil production capacity at 28.04 million B/D, sustainable capacity at 27.44 million B/D. Subtracting CIA's estimates for Iraq and Kuwait left OPEC capacities of 22.34 million B/D available and 21.74 million B/D sustainable.

Immediately after the invasion, then, the market could see that during the fourth quarter of 1990, at the start of the Northern Hemisphere winter, the free world would need 55.3 million B/D. It could assume that the then-dismantling Communist world would be a net exporter, albeit a diminishingly significant one. So it could add non-OPEC production, OPEC crude at estimated available production capacity, OPEC gas liquids, net exports from the crumbling Communist world, and processing gains to arrive at a total supply figure, which came to 53 million B/D in August.

That is 2.3 million B/D less than the best available estimate for what the world would need in fourth quarter 1990. Stocks certainly could not fill a gap of that magnitude. In August, then, the market could look forward to a period in which supply would work as a constraint on demand, the reverse of the situation it faced in July. In August, in other words, the market very properly saw shortage and began immediately to respond. Under the conditions prevailing in August 1990, and until the market completed its adjustment a few months later, the question "Where's the shortage?" was naive in the extreme. The shortage, to the extent that a freely functioning market ever allows one to exist, was at hand.

The Shortage Shrinks

Shortages never last. The market demands surplus. And the market began immediately to recreate the surplus that Saddam Hussein destroyed when he sent his troops into Kuwait.

By the end of August, IEA had pared 800,000 B/D from its projection of fourth-quarter demand outside centrally planned economies. Prices, after all, had jumped. And IEA trimmed its estimate of fourth quarter, non-OPEC supply to 28.7 million B/D, dropping total supply with OPEC producing at then-current estimates of capacity without Iraq and Kuwait to 52.9 million B/D. But the drop in anticipated demand remained eight times the supply decline. In just one month's time, the market had adjusted to the extent that the projected deficit in fourth quarter supply had fallen by 700,000 B/D to 1.6 million B/D.

Irrepressibly, the adjustment continued, precluding the "physical shortages" that politicians demanded to see as a validation for higher prices. The motivation for the adjustment was, of course, concern for replacement supply.

Ultimately, fourth quarter 1990 free world demand amounted to 1.2 million B/D less than what had been projected for the period just prior to the Iraqi invasion. The invasion turned supply into the market's main constraint; prices rose and demand fell accordingly. It was, to repeat, a classic response. And it did not exclude supply, which increased by more than anyone thought possible.

In its December *Oil Market Report,* IEA reported non-OPEC production up 200,000 B/D from earlier estimates and OPEC production up 3.9 million B/D. The OPEC gains came from Saudi Arabia, 2.6 million B/D; Venezuela, 400,000 B/D; the United Arab Emirates and Libya, 300,000 B/D each; and Nigeria and Iran, 200,000 B/D each.

By January 1, OECD crude stocks had reached 3.424 billion bbl, their highest level since 1982. Exporters were holding 50–60 million bbl of crude that they could not sell. IEA in January revised its estimate of December OECD inventory changes from a 500,000 B/D drawdown to a 200,000 B/D build.

It is obvious, in retrospect, that a huge market adjustment had turned a shortage back into surplus by the end of 1990. But a huge question remained: Would the inevitable start of hostilities damage more Persian Gulf oil fields and remove more oil from international trade? Given the outcome of the allied counteroffensive, it is easy to forget that world opinion, up until the ground offensive began, gave the Iraqi military at least even odds for successfully defending its Kuwaiti conquest.

When allied air strikes against Iraq began on January 16, therefore, oil prices jumped. On the U.S. Gulf Coast, West Texas Intermediate crude spot prices leapt by $6–$7/bbl to touch $40 before plummeting later in the day to $32 once the safety of Saudi production facilities seemed certain. On the New York Mercantile Exchange, crude futures for February delivery closed January 16 at $32/bbl, up $1.93, before reports of the war's start. The next day the price fell to $20.30/bbl. Forward Brent blend closed at $30/bbl on January 16 (up $2) in London, then fell to $20.75/bbl the following day.

In the middle of all this, the IEA, which in October had refused to follow the United States in making token volumes available from strategic storage to signal availability of extra supply, announced an emergency plan to make 2.5 million B/D of strategically stored oil and other supplemental fuel supplies available to the market. President Bush ordered sale of 33.75 million bbl from the U.S. strategic reserve. By then, of course, the market had made it painfully clear that the last thing it wanted was more oil.

And then there was the magnanimity of U.S. oil companies that, expecting another retail price run-up, froze prices in one of the most ironic public relations backfires in history. The companies' usual political detractors had their hoots about "price-fixing," but no one cared much. Gasoline was cheap again, the market had the spare capacity that it demanded, and Saddam's troops were in full retreat.

The market had done its part, as it always will when allowed to adjust to crises. Next time, perhaps, energy regulators and oil company executives will display more faith in the process.

THE ROLE OF FUTURES MARKETS

Absence of price and market controls was not the only element of the Gulf crisis and war that distinguished it from past market upsets. This time, well-developed forward and futures markets made price information continuously available and, more importantly, discouraged the hoarding that characteristically aggravates crisis price movements.

Because of the market's inherent concern for replacement supply, it is quite normal for inventories to build whenever supplies seem threatened. This happens throughout the distribution chain, even at the retail level. Anticipating future gasoline price increases, for example, motorists tend to fill their vehicle fuel tanks and to keep them full until they believe prices have peaked. In the wake of any supply interruption, some buildup will appear in stock numbers regularly reported, such as those of the API and IEA. But those numbers do not tell the whole story because they exclude secondary and tertiary inventories. Buildups there appear as a demand increase not manifest in actual consumption, which is extremely difficult to measure. Thus, in a supply crisis, the numbers traditionally reflect a demand surge, as measured by deliveries from primary storage. After a while, demand subsides as two things occur: Secondary and tertiary stocks reach practical capacity, and rising prices discourage actual consumption.

This happened during the Gulf crisis, but the phenomenon ended soon after the invasion. There are two reasons for the fleeting nature of the hoarding period. One is that hoarding was under way even before Iraq invaded Kuwait. Tensions within OPEC, it must be remembered, were very high in June and July. There was much pressure within the exporters' group to trim production and raise the crude price. Market participants had good cause for uncertainty: the Iraqi belligerence, OPEC's irrational agreement, the deliberate overproduction by Kuwait in the face of slumping prices. The OPEC agreement at least signaled the desire for higher prices, even if the announced strategy did not suit the intention. Someone had to cut production—or somehow force someone else to do so.

Enough market participants sensed change to begin buying for storage. By the end of August 1990, IEA was estimating a third-quarter demand increase of 3.5% from year-earlier levels in the OECD due to a secondary and tertiary stock build in July and early August. IEA did not believe that the buildup lasted through all of August.

Early hoarding also seems evident in Energy Information Administration data for U.S. gasoline demand, which increased by more than 1.2 million B/D to 8.6 million B/D the week after Iraq's invasion, then fell to less than 7.1 million B/D the week ending August 17. Apparently, motorists topped their tanks in anticipation of a gasoline price surge. The price increase never materialized in proportion to the crude price rise. According to API, in the six weeks preceding the crisis, spot crude prices rose by the equivalent of 11¢/gal, while spot gasoline prices rose 2¢/gal, and retail prices did not rise at all. During the week of the invasion, spot crude and gasoline prices each rose by 30¢/gal, then dropped 5¢/gal the following week. By August 10, the crude spot price was 23¢/gal higher than its level of mid-June. The retail gasoline price hike during the period amounted to only 14¢/gal. The rest came out of refiners' margins, which turns to bunk the charges of price gouging at the gasoline pump.

So there was a brief period of hoarding, but it ended long before it became obvious that production would come forth to replace lost Iraqi and Kuwaiti crude and that demand would shrink enough to moderate requirements for new supply. In fact, hoarding was an insignificant factor in the market's response to the Gulf crisis. The existence of an active futures market made this so.

For many months before this period of heightened tension capped by the Iraqi invasion, futures markets had been in contango. Too much crude was being produced relative to immediate consumption; stocks were building. A contango, of course, can encourage the process. With forward prices higher than prompt levels—or, in the futures market, with "out" month contracts higher than their "near" month counterparts—storage can look better than futures contracts as a source of future supply. The incentive depends on other factors such as interest rates, market margin requirements, and size of the contango.

Just before the Iraqi invasion, the contango narrowed by some measures and disappeared by others. Tensions were building in OPEC, doubts grew about future supply, and, as we have seen, purchases for storage increased. Prices for crude for immediate delivery and for near-month futures contracts slipped above those for deliveries dated further into the future. The market, in other words, shifted from contango to backwardation.

Table 11–1 depicts the shift. It shows the relationship between New York Mercantile Exchange one-month (near) and six-month (forward) contracts for light, sweet crude. This is a very rough way to assess contango/backwardation relationships, but it highlights the shift and relies on futures market data that are as close as the nearest financial newspaper.

Important points to note are the shrinkage of the contango in the last half of July, then the shift to backwardation in the first week of August. As can be seen, the size of the backwardation varied, reaching nearly $10/bbl early in November.

There are, of course, explanations for the shift beyond what has been presented here. The existence of the dramatic change and its influence in the market are what are important to this discussion.

So what was the influence of a backwardated futures market? Simply put: moderation of the strong tendency to hoard in a crisis. Backwardation discourages purchasing for inventory. If a refiner can buy a six-month futures contract for $7/bbl less than he can buy crude for immediate delivery, why would he buy spot crude in excess of his current needs and store it for half a year? Of course, he might not buy the futures contract either if he thinks spot prices will fall by more than $7/bbl in the next six months.

Backwardation did not prevent a stock build; it was not the only factor in the market, just a new one in comparison with prior crises when a well-developed futures market did not exist. As we have seen, the strong stock draw everyone naturally thought would

TABLE 11-1
THE FUTURES MARKET SWITCHES POSITIONS*

Week beginning	One-month	Six-month	Contango	Backwardation
		—Dollars per barrel—		
May 7	18.70	19.91	1.21	
May 14	19.19	20.22	1.03	
May 21	17.94	19.93	1.99	
May 28	17.74	20.02	2.28	
June 4	16.84	19.07	2.23	
June 11	17.13	19.18	2.05	
June 18	16.26	18.83	2.57	
June 25	17.08	19.01	1.93	
July 2	16.62	18.60	1.98	
July 9	17.56	19.59	2.03	
July 16	18.89	20.81	1.92	
July 23	20.36	21.36	1.00	
July 30	22.01	22.65	0.64	
Aug. 6	25.84	24.80		1.04
Aug. 13	27.13	25.18		1.95
Aug. 20	30.21	27.32		2.89
Aug. 27	26.96	25.05		1.91
Sept. 3	30.09	26.96		3.13
Sept. 10	31.13	27.39		3.74
Sept. 17	34.07	28.86		5.21
Sept. 24	38.70	31.83		6.87
Oct. 1	36.66	31.32		5.34
Oct. 8	39.63	32.63		7.00
Oct. 15	36.83	30.59		6.24
Oct. 22	31.22	26.56		4.66
Oct. 29	34.73	28.63		6.10
Nov. 5	33.86	27.89		9.97
Nov. 12	31.41	27.04		4.37
Nov. 19	30.49	26.22		4.27
Nov. 26	32.17	30.47		1.70
Dec. 3	28.02	24.44		3.58
Dec. 10	26.33	22.97		3.36
Dec. 17	26.83	22.97		3.86
Dec. 24	27.27	23.28		3.99
Dec. 31	26.33	22.96		3.37

*Prices of futures contracts for light, sweet crude traded on the New York Mercantile Exchange.
Source: Author's calculations based on *Oil & Gas Journal* internal price records.

be necessary actually turned into an inventory build by the end of 1990. Notwithstanding backwardated futures markets, new supplies and diminished demand—products of the August-September price spurt—had recreated a physical oversupply. Markets remained nervous nevertheless because no one yet could know the extent to which the imminent war would threaten production facilities in Saudi Arabia and elsewhere.

Free of price and consumption controls, the market would have effected its classic adjustment with or without futures trading. But the futures market provided a real-time gauge of market conditions, which in turn improved the quality of decisions of market participants all along the distribution chain. It is common to hear complaints that the futures market increased price volatility. But these are based on the zig-zag tracks that futures prices make in the course of any trading day. Without futures trading, cash market prices might indeed have followed a similarly irregular course; there simply would have been no way to pull all the information into one place to see what happened.

Moreover, by providing a mechanism to hedge and to buy crude and products now for delivery later, the futures market discouraged panic buying for storage. In that sense it can be said to have moderated price volatility in the Persian Gulf crisis. Economic historians can argue over the finer points of that assertion. What is certain is that a well-developed market in futures contracts and, no doubt, less-centralized trading in forward contracts and derivatives, helped the market adjust with minimum economic disruption to what was a serious disruption in supply.

The only people who now ask "Where's the shortage?" are those who still do not understand what happened.

REFERENCES

1. All data and historical information in this chapter come from various issues of *Oil & Gas Journal* published in weeks before and during the Persian Gulf crisis.

CHAPTER TWELVE

CONCLUSION: ENERGY CHOICES

The petroleum market works. As much as does any other commodity, oil abides by the law of supply and demand. The process can be complex and confusing, but it is always comprehensible. This book has attempted to provide the information essential to making basic sense of the petroleum market's fascinating machinations.

Little has been said about other forms of primary energy: coal, natural gas, hydro and nuclear power, and the more-exotic renewables such as wind, sunlight, and ocean tides. The book, after all, is about oil. Nevertheless, oil exists in a broader world and must compete with the other forms of energy that do, indeed, abound. Closed system that it is, the petroleum market competes for share of a broader energy market.

Oil companies seek reserves in all types of climate. Here the Kulluk drilling unit tests the Pitsiulak A-05 oil discovery in the Canadian Beaufort Sea for Gulf Canada Resources Inc. in July 1984. In the foreground is the Miscaroo ice-breaking support vessel. Photo by Ranson Photographers, Edmonton, Alberta, courtesy of Gulf Canada Resources Ltd. The Kulluk, which Gulf Canada proposed to sell in 1993, specializes in arctic drilling.

It has performed well in this competition. In the United States and worldwide, oil in recent years has accounted for about 40% of all energy consumed. No other source of energy comes close to oil's market share performance, although the petroleum share has been shrinking. Such a pattern is normal in a growing market with a clearly dominant sector or producer.

Arguing the relative benefits of one fuel vs. another makes for popular political sport but is usually pointless. Market figures speak for themselves. People who pay money for energy make the decisions that matter, and the market figures reflect their choices, which ultimately reflect economic choices. These choices are shaped—or contorted, as the case may be—by political strictures in effect at any given time. This book has tried to stress that political strictures that do not comport with basic economic law, strictures that ignore simple relationships between supply, demand, and price, ultimately fail. Economic forces triumph in the end.

The economic forces that guide energy choices thus are periodically resistible but irrepressible over time. That is why efforts to control prices, whether they are grounded in the interests of consumers or producer cartels, inevitably fail. Price manipulations generate self-destructive supply and demand distortions.

Whether governments have come to understand the folly of state market interventions is open to question. Since the early 1980s, price decontrol has been the worldwide trend. This has been the case even in developing producer nations, which characteristically face strong internal pressures to subsidize petroleum product consumption with the bounty provided by crude oil production. Still, as Chapter 11 showed, consuming nation politicians do not shrink from calling for more price controls when market changes raise prices. Had controls been in place in the last half of 1990, the market could not have adjusted as quickly and efficiently as it did to the jolt it sustained in the Persian Gulf crisis. And if officials in charge of strategic inventories had been quicker to recognize shortage in the terms applied by market participants, the adjustment could have been smoother still. Efficiency of the petroleum market still has its doubters. For them, market history of 1990–91 should be instructive. Sequential reading of International Energy Agency's *Monthly Oil Market Reports* through the course of the Gulf crisis is all that should be necessary.

Alas, official petroleum market manipulation has hardly fallen from political fashion. The emphasis has simply shifted from price to demand. According to a quickly developing political belief, the world uses too much oil. Disciples of this belief seldom say much about efficiencies; for example, the relationships between energy consumption and economic growth. And assertions that the world uses too much oil presuppose some acceptable level of consumption, yet few who make the assertions suggest what the acceptable level might be. The fact is that any attempt to define such an optimum level of oil consumption outside the context of markets would amount to little more than an exercise in political cosmetics.

Using less oil, whatever that means, has become a political Holy Grail, nevertheless. It has donned the cloak of morality, implying that using oil is a bad thing to do. The resulting effort to set the world right has produced the interesting shift in political priorities mentioned above. Where before politics endeavored to limit consumer prices, it now tries to limit consumption, usually by forcing consumers to pay more for oil than they did before. From the consumer's perspective, this represents a shift from one side of the argument to the other. Viewed against the history of petroleum politics, it presents a telling paradox: Price increases imposed by government are acceptable; those resulting from the workings of a free market in times of stress are not.

REINVENTING
ECONOMICS

Proponents of the less-oil-consumption-at-any-cost evangel often attempt to reinvent economics to rationalize their position. They do so in two broad ways. The more sophisticated rationalization centers on the theory of external costs. The less-sophisticated rationalization is probably the more persuasive. It says that the world ought to use less oil because it is depleting a finite resource. Both rationalizations deserve closer examination than they usually receive.

EXTERNAL COSTS

The theory of external costs, as it is applied to petroleum says that oil generates costs not reflected in market prices. These costs fall into two categories: security and environmental.

Major oil-consuming nations have demonstrated their willingness to defend foreign sources of petroleum with military force. Mobilizations, such as the one that expelled Iraqi troops from Kuwait in 1991, cost billions of dollars. They also kill people. These are external costs, as are the costs of maintaining an army capable of mobilizing in defense of oil supplies when needed. According to the popular theory, the price of oil should reflect these externalities.

But how? And how much?

Measuring external security costs is difficult, if not impossible. Troops deployed for the liberation of Kuwait would have generated costs even if they had remained in garrison or on reserve status. To be sure, the costs of deployed troops exceed those of troops staying home. But what is the increment? Whatever it might be, it must be reduced to the extent that Persian Gulf countries compensated their defenders in cash, which Kuwait and Saudi Arabia did. And the discount should be enlarged to whatever degree Gulf exporters may have expressed their gratitude in the form of deliberate price moderation, as some observers suspect that they did.

On the other hand, garrison costs ought to figure somewhere in an accounting of external cost. Idle military forces have deterrent power. Presence of consuming-nation military capability has an undeniable if imperfect tranquilizing effect on the volatile Middle East. But then that capability has deterrent power outside the petroleum-producing world, too. So how much of the cost of basic military readiness ought to be apportioned to oil in this calculation of external cost? Maybe oil prices, in line with the popular theory, should reflect basic readiness costs at all times, then contain some sort of war-time premium when troops move to defend foreign suppliers.

But wait: Nations maintain military capability in order to protect all of their interests—not just oil—everywhere, not just in oil-producing regions. How are they to distinguish between defense costs related to petroleum and those not?

Moreover, if the external cost theory is valid in relation to security and oil, then defense spending ought to vary in proportion to the degree of a country's dependency upon oil from abroad. Yet Japan, nearly 100% dependent upon foreign oil, maintains a military that is at best modest by international standards. The United States, with import dependency less than half that of Japan's, maintains and pays for the most powerful military force in the world.

There is certainly nothing to suggest that the U.S. defense budget would be any smaller if oil import dependency were 25% instead of 47%, as it was in 1992.

The problems of measuring oil's environmental external costs are no less daunting. Oil falls subject to a host of environmentalist charges and certainly is guilty of some of them. At times it leaks or spills onto the ground or into water, although spillers often pay cleanup costs, which should then not be counted as external. Petroleum evaporation and combustion contribute to air pollution, although the extent varies from region to region and in any case is subject to scientific question. Air pollution in turn contributes to health problems for some people, who might be said to bear much of the burden of petroleum's external costs in their health bills. But how much of their health problems are directly attributable to petroleum?

Experts cannot agree, of course. In fact, some air pollution is tolerable in terms of its effect on health, although opinions differ on where to draw the risk line. Yet proponents of the external cost theory often make it sound as though any contribution to air pollution constitutes a cost that ought to be compensated for in oil price. And what about controversial environmental theories such as global warming, in which one side sees imminent hazard and the other sees no phenomenon at all? Costs cannot be validly assessed on something so uncertain.

The purpose here is not to argue the global warming question and other environmental issues but to raise questions about claims that external environmental costs can be measured with sufficient certainty to make them a part of what people pay for oil. And if they are, who then is to say that "external benefits" ought not be subtracted from price? Such benefits might include the non-petroleum trade opportunities that open up as a result of two nations dealing in oil. There even is a serious if popularly ignored scientific theory that says the world for hundreds of millennia has been starved of carbon dioxide, the greenhouse gas that inculpates fossil fuels in the global warming issue. According to this theory the carbon dioxide buildup now in progress will make the world more luxuriant with plant life and help resolve global hunger. If so, ought that not be construed as an external benefit, and oil prices cut accordingly?

The problems of external cost theory should be obvious. External costs are almost impossible to measure and provide weighty opportunity for analytical mischief. By the nature of their being "external," they can be added to price only by way of taxation. Most principles of honest government hold that taxes ought not to be increased on the basis of anything so uncertain and subjective.

Defense capabilities must, of course, be maintained. Environmental protection is important. Nothing here is intended to detract from these very proper concerns of governments and nations. But pursuit of these concerns are matters of political choice. Governments at their best operate in those realms where individual exertions are ineffective. Defense is certainly one such realm. Environmental protection and remediation are, too, because a majority of individuals probably can always agree on generalities in these areas but seldom on specifics and costs. One person's "external cost" is another's indispensable benefit. Heat produced by such frictions might, by some ways of thinking, constitute a transaction, but it certainly is not economics.

A sovereign body must decide how much defense it wants and weigh that desire against how much it can afford. It must do the same with regard to environmental protection. If a nation so fears global warming that it feels compelled to curb oil consumption despite scientific doubts about the need for such sacrifice, then so be it. That is politics. To try to rationalize the move by resorting to the hazy economics of external costs is, however, to strain credibility in the effort.

DEPLETION ANXIETIES

The popular urge not to consume oil out of concern for the finite nature of the petroleum resource reflects a charming thrift. The squirrel has only so many nuts put back for winter, after all; he has to make them last.

The squirrel, however, knows how many nuts he had in the nest when winter began. And he did not have to pay money for them.

Yes, the petroleum resource is finite. As Chapter 5 pointed out, however, no one knows how finite the resource is. The bottom of the tub is nowhere in view, and technology keeps making the tub deeper.

Does this mean consumers are free to go on an oil consumption binge? Certainly not. But the consumption restraint is not some notion about the world's last barrel of oil. The restraint is price. Unbridled consumption is impossible as long as prices are free to change along with relationships in supply and demand.

To delay exhaustion of an indisputably exhaustible resource for as long as is possible certainly seems sensible. But why should this be so? Is there really an advantage in prolonging the life of the petroleum resource? If there is, how much should we be willing to pay for it?

Answers would be easier if petroleum were the only energy source available to humankind. To extend the metaphor, however, this squirrel eats more than nuts. When petroleum is gone, the next best thing will replace it. As long as they remain inclined to work, people will have energy, and—as long as they are free to do so—they will choose the energy source that best suits their economic needs.

This far in time from petroleum exhaustion, the choice is one of process. One process is a natural economic and geologic progression, in which the cheapest and most efficient energy sources are used and depleted first. Eventually, scarcity raises their prices, and the elevated values bring heretofore marginal energy sources into the economic sphere. Under present technology, this looks like a progression from low-cost, nonrenewable energies such as oil, natural gas, and coal to higher cost nonrenewables such as tar sands and shale oil, and eventually to renewables such as solar, wind, and hydrogen. If politics were different, nuclear power would fit more solidly in the spectrum than it now does. And technological changes can and probably will change the order somewhat.

The alternative process is mandated priority, in which consumption of the cheapest, most efficient energy is somehow limited and supplemented by some other source of energy rendered competitive with some sort of subsidy. The United States tried this approach on a massive scale in the late 1970s with the Synthetic Fuels Corporation. The effort, designed to make a total of $88 billion in tax and other advantages available to unconventional fuels, failed. On a smaller scale, the country uses the approach in different forms with tax credits for natural gas from low-porosity reservoirs and coal seams and for grain-derived ethanol blended into gasoline.

In practice, governments apply some combination of these processes for a variety of reasons, some good and some bad. The question here is whether governments should encourage supplementation of petroleum by less-efficient, more-costly fuels for the sole purpose of delaying exhaustion of the petroleum resource.

The economic answer is no. The strategy is costly. It forces consumers to pay more than they otherwise would for energy. Resulting inefficiencies inevitably corrode a country's economic growth. Benefits, if any, are impossible to measure. Petroleum resources might last longer, although no one can tell how much longer because the point of exhaustion is beyond view now. Then again, petroleum resources might not last any longer at all. Measures taken to delay resource exhaustion might, and often do, have the effect of simply leaving otherwise producible oil in the ground, while something more expensive prematurely gains share of the total energy market. The petroleum resource never gets exhausted; it simply gets locked away forever. The only benefits in this proposition are those that accrue to the politically favored fuels. Everyone else pays, cursed to use less than optimum fuel.

There are other considerations, of course. There are places, for example, where environmental delicacies outweigh the value of whatever petroleum reserves may lie underground, although the argument suffers from overuse in modern politics. And the notion of deliberate delay in resource development—or outright nondevelopment—should not be confused with near-term production constraint for the sake of balancing markets, which is something quite different.

The aim here is to assert something that differs from what has perhaps become an excessive amount of worry about the rate at which we, as people needing energy in order to perform work, are using up the petroleum resource. The worry needs to be tempered with the question whether we are using up the resource in ways that assure that, in the end, we get it all.

CREATING
ECONOMIC
VALUE

Petroleum is a gift of nature. It exists to be used. It ought to be used wisely.

Petroleum left in the ground has no value. Unless petroleum is developed, produced, and processed, petroleum is a worthless gift.

At another extreme, petroleum burned frivolously depreciates the gift. Much is said these days about "wasting" energy, especially oil. Indeed, much oil is burned frivolously and therefore wasted—but not in the usual sense of the allegation. Oil is burned frivolously when it is consumed under less than optimum economic terms; when, that is, anyone along the market's containment system is denied the opportunity to earn competitive profits. The United States burned oil frivolously when it controlled prices of old domestic crude oil and oil products during the 1970s. Developing oil-producing nations burn oil frivolously when they subsidize domestic product prices, as many of them do. Price controls and product subsidies create demand beyond that which would exist if the market functioned freely and prevent the full realization of oil's economic value at some point in the distribution chain. This is waste in the same sense that oil deliberately left in the ground is waste.

Oil has to do with wealth—and not just the riches of Texas tycoons or Middle Eastern sheiks. Energy is a vital ingredient of economic growth. Oil, because of its high energy content per unit of volume and weight, is one of energy's most important forms. To purposefully proscribe an economy's access to optimum energy inputs is to create inefficiencies that become manifest as costs.

There may be good reasons for undertaking such burdens. The choices, again, are political. What governments should not do is pretend that the costs do not exist or impose them for invalid reasons. The decision to limit use of oil is a decision to raise costs of a crucial economic input. A nation ignores that economic reality at its peril.

Moreover, deliberate limits on oil consumption have consequences outside the countries that implement them. For many countries, oil production represents an indispensable or sole source of wealth. Countries like these understandably view "off-oil" policies of major consuming countries with perplexed disdain. In the early 1990s, a global fault line was developing over this issue. On one side was the developing world, with economic growth characteristically based on exploitation of natural resources. Many developing countries were rapidly opening their petroleum prospects to international exploration and development. The general hope was to take advantage of foreign technology and capital in resource development and to use retained proceeds for development of nonresource industries. On the other side of this fault line were already industrialized countries, their manufacturing infrastructures in place, their economies increasingly oriented to adding value to raw materials and intermediate products and less to producing the raw materials themselves. It was from these countries that off-oil proposals most often emanated.

To the developing world, such clamoring for an end to the Petroleum Age seemed premature and confrontational. Were developing countries to be denied their turns to exploit natural resources and industrialize? Indeed, when then-Senator Albert Gore, destined to become Vice President of the United States, blithely wrote that his country should phase out the internal combustion engine within a quarter of a century, he seemed to be ignoring much about the rest of the world, not to mention his own country.

Developed countries nevertheless have valid concerns that developing nations should heed. Environmental politics may often exaggerate the consequences of petroleum use, but the wretched congestion and pollution in cities where gasoline sells for a fraction of its economic value lead to valid conclusions that something must be done. Furthermore, it is one of the great tragedies of the twentieth century that some petroleum-producing countries, such as Saddam Hussein's Iraq, have chosen to spend their oil wealth not on productive economic infrastructure but on menacing buildups of military might.

It may, as this chapter has suggested, stretch analysis to the breaking point to hope that oil prices can somehow cover all the environmental and military contingencies that forever encumber petroleum. External costs make for fancy intellectualizing but poor economics. But petroleum has undeniable inconveniences that call for tough political decision-making. The emphasis this book places on economics is in no way intended to deny or diminish petroleum's political dimension. The message here is that petroleum's economic and political dimensions can be much better distinguished and turned into constructive policy than they have so been so far in history.

THE FUTURE

T he world will not quit using oil. The Petroleum Age is nowhere near its end, much as some interest groups would like it to be.

The market works. The containment system is in place. Turning the wishful thinking that underlies "off-oil" strategies into functional reality would clash with economic reality. Economic forces, as history shows, have a way of prevailing over politics in the end.

Are we, then, somehow at the mercy of our need for petroleum? Is growth in air pollution inevitable? Must tanker oil spills be tolerated with some cruel frequency? Will the oil-consuming world have to commit military forces time and again to defense of its crucial sources of crude oil?

No, we are not at the mercy of our need for petroleum. We are in possession of a gift, a valuable tool of economic progress, which is ours to use or not, wisely or otherwise. Using the gift wisely best suits the most people—as long as most people want to pursue constructive work. And we can make use of the gift without ruining nature.

Those who make contrary claims about petroleum and the environment ignore an important factor in the economic equation: technology. Oil consumption is a much cleaner proposition now than it was just a decade ago, and it becomes more so all the time. The United States has demonstrated that a country determined to do so can mitigate air pollution as an act of political will. With a combination of automobile engine design changes and fuel performance regulations it has reduced vehicle emissions overall and brought all but a few of its cities into federally specified tolerances for the major air pollutants. Further improvements, however costly and technically challenging they may be, will result from Clean Air Act amendments enacted in 1990. Other countries are adopting or considering comparable efforts. Significant pollution reductions would be possible if countries with large gasoline subsidies would let market prices moderate consumption. Similarly, improved technology and regulation can keep major tanker accidents from being an inevitable fact of economic life. Requirements for a better future are commitment to technology, recognition of the constructive potential of markets, acceptance of economic reality, and a proper balance between political will and regulatory restraint.

If history properly instructs, the answer to the question of whether military action represents an unavoidable byproduct of petroleum consumption must be yes. Countries have fought for oil throughout history, whether for control of reserves and production or in defense of important sources of supply. Oil is wealth from the aspects of both production and consumption. Where there is oil, there is national interest; when national interests clash, there sometimes is war.

The hope must lie in vastly improved diplomacy and sophisticated leadership. Mandatory reductions in oil consumption will not get the job done. Such reductions by one set of countries would simply transfer economic and, possibly, military advantages, to all others. Such a shift by itself might be sufficiently destabilizing to promote conflict. What diplomacy and leadership might accomplish are moderation of competitive tensions over supply, on the one hand, and orientation of producers toward prosperity instead of power, on the other. It should not go unnoted that, as anyone in the oil industry can attest, petroleum provides a rich variety of opportunities for cultural exchange. Is it naive to hope that this can work to advance peaceful relations among peoples and nations? Maybe this should be another of those "external" benefits proposed in opposition to external costs earlier in this chapter.

Wise use of the petroleum gift means production and consumption in accordance with economic laws and reasonable political imperatives—domestic and international. If markets are allowed to work, the world need not fear shortage. If regulations are sound and proper environmental ethics firmly in place across the market, the world need not fear natural destruction. What the world should fear most are inefficiency and unfounded anxiety about technology. An unfortunate but defining characteristic of our world is still human deprivation, the only antidotes for which are economic development and technical progress. Global healing requires work, the immediate precursor of which is energy. The process is too important to be made to use anything but the best.

Someday the limit of the petroleum resource will come into sight. At that point scarcity will begin to play a role in the market.

The concern for future supply will scan wider horizons, settling first, perhaps, on exotic hydrocarbons and increasingly on renewables.

This, at least, is the vision. It is a vision of eventual transition from petroleum and other nonrenewable energy sources to renewables, a transition that can be smooth and painless as long as it is governed in accordance with economic laws. Those laws dictate careful and comprehensive use of the world's lavish gift of petroleum.

For the sake of all who seek better life, freedom from hunger, and hope for the future, we must use petroleum to the full extent of what economics defines as its value. The questions need never be, where's the shortage? but, what value have we added to this wondrous treasure? and, how have we used petroleum to improve our habitat? Economics can point the way. People must provide the answers.

All that is at stake in the energy choices of today's industrial elite is the chance for maximum welfare for the most people tomorrow and greater prosperity for all the world's people after that. We must choose wisely.

INDEX